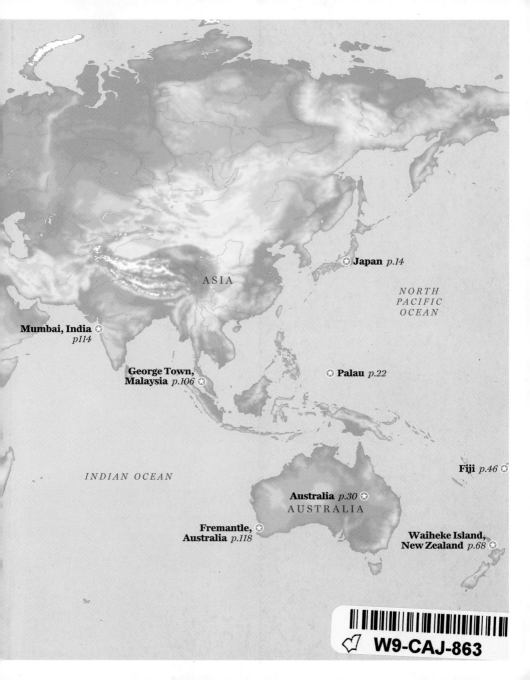

ASIA

NORTH
PACIFIC
OCEAN

☆ **Japan** *p.14*

Mumbai, India ☆
p114

☆ **Palau** *p.22*

George Town,
Malaysia *p.106* ☆

INDIAN OCEAN

Fiji *p.46* ☆

Australia *p.30* ☆
AUSTRALIA

Fremantle,
Australia *p.118* ☆

Waiheke Island,
New Zealand *p.68* ☆

◁ **W9-CAJ-863**

LONELY PLANET'S

BEST IN TRAVEL

2016

Contents

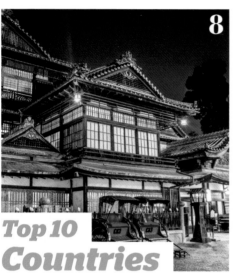

8

Top 10
Countries

50

Top 10
Regions

BEST IN
TRAVEL
2016

92

Top 10
Cities

134

Top
Travel lists

The Best in Travel Promise

Where is the best place to visit right now?

This is the most hotly contested topic at Lonely Planet and dominates more conversations than any other. As self-confessed travel geeks, our staff collectively rack up hundreds of thousands of miles each year, exploring almost every destination on the planet in the process.

Where is the best place to visit right now? We ask everyone at Lonely Planet, from our authors and editors all the way to our online family of bloggers and tweeters. And each year they come up with hundreds of places that are buzzy right now, offer new things for travellers to see or do, or are criminally overlooked and underrated.

Amid fierce debate, the list is whittled down by our panel of travel experts to just 10 countries, 10 regions and 10 cities. Each is chosen for its topicality, unique experiences and 'wow' factor. We don't just report on the trends, we set them – helping you get there before the crowds do.

Put simply, what remains in the pages that follow is the cream of this year's travel picks, courtesy of Lonely Planet: 10 countries, 10 regions, 10 cities and a host of travel lists to inspire you to explore for yourself.

So what are you waiting for?

BEST IN
TRAVEL
2016

Lonely Planet's
Top 10
Countries

SEAN PAVONE © SHUTTERSTOCK

CATCH A GLIMPSE OF
THE MIGHTY LEOPARD
IN BOTSWANA'S CHOBE
NATIONAL PARK

BEST IN
TRAVEL
2016

Botswana

Botswana is a unique destination: an unusual combination of desert and delta that draws an immense concentration of wildlife

ADVENTURE | ACTIVITIES | CULTURE

Population: **2 million**

Foreign visitors per year: **2.1 million**

Capital: **Gaborone**

Languages: **Setswana, Kalanga, English**

Major industry: **diamonds, copper, nickel**

Unit of currency: **pula (P)**

Cost index: **mid-range camp per night P6048 (US$600), flight transfers P1512-2016 (US$150-200), bottle of beer P25 (US$2.5), litre of petrol P10 (US$0.99)**

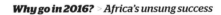

Why go in 2016? > *Africa's unsung success*

In 2016 Botswana will celebrate its 50th year of independence. So what, you may say. What's there to shout about? Well, quite a lot really. Not least the longest continuous multi-party democracy on the continent, a progressive social outlook (Botswana was one of the first countries to offer free anti-retroviral drugs to its citizens in 2002), minimal corruption, a healthy and enlightened tourism industry and a fast-growing economy since independence. The country's journey from abject poverty in 1966 to become one of Africa's most stable and thriving societies is hugely inspiring and, no doubt, deserves a proverbial pat on the back.

But that's not all. Botswana is a unique destination: an unusual combination of desert and delta that draws an immense concentration of wildlife. It is wild, pristine and expansive. Seventeen percent of the country is dedicated to national parks, many of them spreading into the vast Transfrontier parks of Kavango-Zambezi and Kgalagadi. This dedication to conserving some of the world's last remaining wildernesses was finally recognised in 2014 when the jewel in Botswana's conservation crown, the Okavango Delta, became Unesco's 1000th World Heritage Site.

Despite this embarrassment of accolades, Botswana remains off the radar for most people. The impression is: it's too expensive, it's too difficult to get to, it doesn't cater for families. But we're here to tell you that's all nonsense. Go now! Go by plane, car or *mokoro* (canoe). Go in the green season or the dry season – it's all great. Go to Vumbura Plains Camp or Jao Camp with tons of cash for the trip of a lifetime or go on a budget to community projects like Tsabong Camel Park and Moremi Gorge. Go as a honeymooning couple to gaze over the dreamy Zibandianja Lagoon in Linyanti or as an adventure junkie to ride horseback through Mashatu Game Reserve. Go as a wildlife enthusiast and track elephants in the mini-Serengeti of Savuti or meerkats on the Makgadikgadi Pans. Go alone to take your guiding qualifications at Okavango Guiding School or with the

kids to experience Ker & Downey's award-winning family safari (Safari Awards 2015). Whatever you do and whenever you go, you won't regret it. Trust us on this one.

Life-changing experiences

Botswana is so full of life-changing experiences it would be easier to list the things that aren't remarkable. Here is a real wilderness that puts you in touch with palpable primitive thrills and fears, whether it's being poled by an African gondolier in a *mokoro* past pods of sunbathing hippos in the Okavango Delta; or feeling the spirit of the

Festivals & events

The annual Toyota 1000 Desert Race held in June on Jwaneng's unforgiving terrain is southern Africa's premier off-road rally. Winners here are guaranteed a place in the prestigious Dakar Rally.

The trans-frontier Tour de Tuli is a hardcore mountain bike race held in August. It traverses unmanicured elephant trails between Botswana, Zimbabwe and South Africa.

If you want to connect with Batswana culture, head to the Maun International Arts Festival held in the small town of Maun in October. This week-long culturefest showcases local poetry, storytelling, painting, jazz and folklore.

BEST IN TRAVEL 2016

first men in the thousand-year-old rock art in the Tsodilo Hills; or in the eerie beauty of Kubu Island's ancient baobabs backlit by incandescent constellations in a vast night sky.

Current craze
So called 'car park pimping'. Thanks to a 30% tax on alcohol and new licensing hours enforcing club closures at 2am, Gaborone's club scene has moved outdoors and hijacked suburban car parks. Here the party continues around makeshift DJ decks with experienced clubbers equipped with personal cool boxes and camping chairs.

Trending topic
Direct flights. For years the government has been clamouring for direct international flights, and the relocation of De Beers' sales office from London to Gaborone (handling about US$6.5-billion worth of rough diamond sales annually) in 2013 has undoubtedly added new pressure. Gaborone's airport and runway have recently been upgraded and similar upgrades are planned for Maun and Kasane. With all the action people are hoping the long-awaited day may come within the next 6 to 12 months.

● *By Paula Hardy*

ELEPHANTS LUMBER PAST A WATERING HOLE IN KWANDO RESERVE

What's hot...
Community projects, eco-accreditation, family travel, Botswana Innovation Hub

...What's not
Mass tourism, hunting (banned in 2014), drink driving, illegal logging

Here is a real wilderness that puts you in touch with palpable primitive thrills and fear

PRACTISE YOUR PEOPLE-DODGING SKILLS
AT SHIBUYA CROSSING – IT'S NICKNAMED
'THE SCRAMBLE' FOR A REASON

Japan

With the government's continued efforts to devalue the Japanese yen, there's no better time to experience the country that pays such vivid tribute to manic modernity and hallowed history

CULTURE   FOOD   VALUE

Population: **126.9 million**
Foreign visitors per year: **13.5 million**
Capital: **Tokyo**
Language: **Japanese**
Major industry: **manufacturing (automobiles, electronics)**
Unit of currency: **yen (¥)**
Cost index: **bowl of ramen noodles ¥700 (US$5.75), mid-range hotel double per night ¥18,000-35,000 (US$150-290), one-way Nozomi bullet train ride from Tokyo to Kyoto ¥13,720 (US$113), whisky highball ¥650 (US$5.35)**

2

Why go in 2016?
> *New horizons in the land of the rising sun*

Even if you've never been to Japan, you probably already know that it ranks number one in the world for that quintessential not-in-Kansas-anymore travel experience. Its cities are expertly crafted odes to futurism where the trains whirr by in the blink of an eye and the towers of metal and glass are bathed in neon light. The countryside, too, feels otherworldly, with all-continents-in-one landscapes that blend alpine peaks with shimmering shores. And everywhere in between are prim wooden temples – the constant reminder that a well of deep-seated traditions hides just beneath the country's enticing veneer of perfection.

Although Japan didn't secure the Olympic bid for 2016, it was resoundingly successful with its application for Tokyo in 2020. And Olympic fever is already apparent in the capital as the city executes an elaborate feat of urban planning that will create a brand new shopping district, an entirely new Olympic village, and – most interestingly – move the much-venerated Tsukiji fish market (which sees over US$20 million in seafood sales each day) to a sparkling new facility that is set to swing open its doors at the end of this year.

As everyone's radioactive paranoia is finally put to rest by honouring five years since the fateful 2011 Tōhoku earthquake and tsunami, and with the government's continued efforts to devalue the Japanese yen, there's no better time to experience the country that pays such vivid tribute to manic modernity and hallowed history.

Life-changing experience

One of the world's most famous pilgrimage routes after the Camino de Santiago is Japan's Kumano Kodō near Osaka. For over a millennium devotees of every ilk – be it farmer or emperor – would walk betwixt hidden *Oji* shrines and forests of haunting trees to reach the three grand worshipping complexes of Kumano. There are a handful of different paths that extend like spokes around the Kii peninsula, but

Festivals & events

For a country that habitually seesaws between hiding and celebrating its notorious sexual appetite, Japan's most procreation-positive festival is held in early April during Kanamara Matsuri. What began in the 1600s as ritualised prayer among prostitutes seeking divine protection against sexually transmitted diseases retains its prophylactic-promoting roots while adding playful penis trinkets (think hats and puppets) and a well-attended parade focused upon a phallic float.

The appropriation of Christmas Day, which isn't technically a national holiday in Japan, borrows from a bizarre assortment of Western traditions. Many would consider it their version of Valentine's Day, when young romantics gather to stroll among dazzling yule-themed light shows and chow down on fried chicken. Kentucky Fried Chicken is the bird of choice, perhaps because Colonel Sanders is a dead ringer for a svelter Santa Claus?

THE SACRED TRAIL OF KUMANO KODŌ REVEALS SHRINES NESTLED AMONG THE FOREST'S ANCIENT TREES

For over a millennium devotees of every ilk would walk betwixt hidden Oji shrines and forests of haunting trees

↑

What's hot...
Momiji-gari, colourful
autumn 'leaf peeping'
Snaggle-teeth
Love hotels
Taking the new bullet
train to Kanazawa

—

What's not
Kyoto's crowds at peak
cherry-blossom season
Braces
Capsule hotels
Taking a taxi anywhere

↓

the goal is united in the act of spiritual penance performed by hikers as they rigorously trek. The preferred route – and also the oldest – is Nakahechi, which starts in the west and travels 30km to the shrines. Unesco officially recognised the network of trails in 2004, and over the last 12 years the walk has seen a steady increase in foreign tourists.

Current craze

Animal cafes. Yes, cat cafes are *so* 2009, and have proliferated across the globe, but in Japan – the genesis country – animal cafes have reached new heights: hobnob with goats, sip tea with a turtle, pose for selfies with owls, and do whisky shots while watching penguins.

Random facts

■ There are over 5.5 million vending machines in Japan selling everything from umbrellas and cigarettes to canned bread and hot noodles.
■ Japan's birth rate has plummeted so significantly that adult nappies (diapers) outsell babies' nappies, which are also sold in vending machines.
■ It is estimated that more paper is used for manga comics than for toilet paper in Japan. (Surprise: both are sold in vending machines as well.)

Most bizarre sight

Cafes where you can tickle owls? Vending machines that sell canned bread? Dentists that help patients accentuate their snaggle-teeth? Take your pick!
● *By Brandon Presser*

HIRE A FORD MUSTANG
AND TAKE TO THE DESERT
HIGHWAYS FOR THE ULTIMATE
AMERICAN ROADTRIP

BEST IN
TRAVEL
2016

USA

Geysers spurt hundreds of feet high, massive canyons split the horizon in two: these are some of the most spectacular and surreal landscapes on the planet

ACTIVITIES · ADVENTURE · EVENTS

Population: **318.9 million**
Foreign visitors per year: **74.7 million**
Capital: **Washington, DC**
Language(s): **English**
Major industry: **manufacturing**
Unit of currency: **US dollar (US$)**
Cost index: **glass of craft beer US$5, hotel double US$70-500, short taxi ride US$12, entry to Yosemite National Park US$30 per car, 15-minute helicopter ride over Grand Canyon US$145**

> **Why go in 2016?** > *America's best idea is better than ever*
Yellowstone, the Badlands, Zion, Shenandoah… Even their names evoke lands of Tolkienesque make-believe. Places where trolls and dragons roam, and magic happens. Step beyond the gates of America's national parks, and you'll soon be thinking old JRR should have broadened the scope of his imagination. Geysers spurt hundreds of feet high, massive canyons split the horizon in two, herds of bison graze in stunning valleys, and giant tree trunks, as ancient as Rome's Colosseum, disappear into the sky. These are some of the most spectacular and surreal landscapes on the planet, and the fact that they are looking much the same as they did at the

birth of this land-grabbing, highway-loving nation, is frankly a miracle. In 2016, the National Park Service (NPS), the government body which protects and maintains America's 59 national parks and hundreds of historic landmarks, is turning 100 years old, and like any great host, this old-timer has been busting a gut to ensure the parks are at their best for the centenary.

It was historian Wallace Stegner who called the national parks 'the best idea we ever had. Absolutely American, absolutely democratic, they reflect us at our best rather than our worst.' These are the country's national treasures; as hallowed and revered as India's golden temples or the castles and cathedrals of Europe. Since its inception the NPS – most recognisable in the wide-brimmed figure of the park ranger – has been busy clearing litter, fighting fires, protecting wildlife, and providing information on everything from the habitat of the American black bear to the geology of Utah's sandstone arches.

This centenary is an occasion that will be marked not by cake and balloons, but by the fruition of billions of dollars of investment and ambitious initiatives that will prepare the NPS for a second

YOSEMITE'S HALF DOME IS A POPULAR CHALLENGE FOR KEEN HIKERS... BUT YOU MIGHT PREFER TO ADMIRE ITS BEAUTY FROM AFAR

Festivals & events

The final match of the National Football League championship is a momentous occasion in any year, but on 7 February 2016, Super Bowl 50 will play out on TV sets across the nation. Expect massive hype, heart-in-your-mouth plays and extravagant half-time celebrations, with or without nipple slippage.

For three weeks in June 2016, the 100th Copa América – one of the world's oldest and most popular sporting events – will be held in cities across the country. Although unlikely to win, all eyes will be on the first-time host USA to bring the party to thousands of Latin American soccer fans.

The Indianapolis Motor Speedway is the highest capacity sports venue in the world and over the last weekend of May it will be packed out as over 400,000 crazed petrolheads make their pilgrimage for the 100th running of the Indy 500 car race.

What's hot...
Deep space,
walkable cities,
'small plate' dining

What's not...
Spying, drones,
oversized portions

century. These range from the physical: clearing trails, improving accessibility, and installing the latest technology, to the inspirational: hosting 'discovery' events, involving thousands of young people in volunteer programs, and promoting enjoyment of the parks to urban communities.

It's serious work. Serious work that has the most wondrous end: discovery of the national parks themselves. Yosemite's mighty granite cliffs and fairy-tale waterfalls, Zion's claustrophobic slot canyons, the steamy swamps of the Everglades, howling wolves, soaring condors, glittering glaciers... There are 340,000 sq km (84.4 million acres) to choose from. As you lace up the hiking boots, just remember to give your thanks to those hardworking folk at the NPS.

Life-changing experience

The world's third-largest nation is a road-tripping paradise. As you take to highways travelled by Thelma and Louise and Bonnie and Clyde, watch the landscape morph from prairie to desert to breathtaking ocean road. On the way, goofy roadside attractions, small-town diners and curious locals are the added spice for the great American road trip.

Trending topic

The election. In 2016, America's first African-American president will step down. As nationwide protests change the way Americans think about politics, this election year promises raging debate, as well as the usual flag flying and amusing (or just plain rude) bumper stickers. Will history be made again with the inauguration of America's first female president?

● *By Dora Whitaker*

THE WHITE SANDS AND AZURE
WATERS OF PALAU ARE THE STUFF
OF GET-AWAY-FROM-IT-ALL DREAMS

BEST IN
TRAVEL
2016

Palau

More than 200 largely unspoilt limestone and volcanic islands are blanketed in tropical and mangrove forest and surrounded by waters teeming with marine life

ACTIVITIES | ADVENTURE | OFF-ROAD

Population: **21,000**

Foreign visitors per year: **147,000**

Capital: **Ngerulmud**

Languages: **Palauan, English**

Major industries: **tourism, subsistence agriculture, fishing**

Unit of currency: **US dollar (US$)**

Cost index: **day's diving US$150, three-course meal US$40, beer US$2.50, bottle of water US$0.80**

Why go in 2016? > The Pacific's greenest secret

Handballed between various foreign powers for centuries, Pacific pipsqueak Palau is charting its own path through the uncertain waters of national independence. While the US still plays Big Daddy, Palau is its own master. In 2014 President Remengesau was named a 'Champion of the Earth' by the United Nations for strengthening the economic and environmental independence of Palau and creating a 100% marine sanctuary of its oceans. His message: 'The environment is our economy. The economy is our environment.'

Collected behind a 110km barrier reef, more than 200 largely unspoilt

A DIVER MEETS A
FRIENDLY NAUTILUS IN
PALAU'S UNDERWATER
WONDERLAND

↑

What's hot...
Diving, sustainable
tourism, underwater
photography

———

What's not...
Dynamite fishing, rising
sea levels, missionaries

↓

limestone and volcanic islands – a
mere eight are inhabited – are
blanketed in tropical and mangrove
forest and surrounded by waters
teeming with marine life. Fairly
constant temperatures and rainfall
mean any time of the year is good
to visit, although it becomes more
typhoon-prone in the back half of the
calendar.

Palau has as much to fear from
rising sea levels and environmental
degradation as any other Pacific
nation, but it's tackling those fears
head-on, and is leading conservation
efforts in the region. Such progressive
thinking makes these islands a
haven for diving and snorkelling
(among the best in the world) as well
as kayaking, sailing and wildlife
watching. The secret is out in East
Asia already, which means Palau
is looking to limit the number of
tourists it can host at a time.

Life-changing experiences
Cutely dubbed an 'underwater
Serengeti', Palau's waters are
stunningly diverse and it's

unquestionably one of the most magical
underwater destinations in the world. Divers and
snorkellers enjoy hundreds of species of fish and
coral, sharks, dolphins, dugongs and turtles, all
attracted by the confluence of nutritive currents
that meets in this corner of the Pacific vastness.

If you prefer to stay above sea level, take an
ocean kayak through the uninhabited archipelago
of the Rock Islands. Almost alien in its beauty,
it's made up of 445 limestone formations
swaddled with verdant green and fringed by reefs.
Nearly 400 species of coral, the world's highest
concentration of marine lakes, the remains of
now-vanished human habitation and the
continuing discovery of new and endemic species
led Unesco to list this as a World Heritage Site.

Current craze

In 1944, the Japanese and Americans fought for three desperate months for control of the island of Peleliu's important airfield. The tragic result was over 10,000 Japanese and 2,000 American casualties, and an island paradise littered with wreckage. Today, many of the rusted tanks, planes, small arms and (highly dangerous) unexploded ordnance that attest to the ferocity of the struggle remain. Tourists, carefully shepherded by expert guides, are increasingly being drawn to this fascinating site, where you can even enter the cave networks left by the Japanese defenders, and find everyday artefacts left behind. This isn't as ghoulish as it may sound: many of the visitors are here to pay respect to fallen relatives, and moves are afoot to preserve the site for its outstanding historical significance.

Trending topic

A 400% year-on-year increase in visitors from China in February 2015 put some noses out of joint in Palau and resulted in a reduction in flights scheduled from China. Palau's pristine environment makes it a popular destination for the Chinese, Korean and Japanese jet set, but locals have complained about a lack of environmental awareness threatening their precious assets.

Most bizarre sight

Jellyfish Lake is an otherworldy lagoon on the uninhabited limestone Rock Island of Eil Malk. Millions of an endemic sub-species of golden jellyfish drift across the marine lake in an east-west migratory pattern that's repeated every day. Such is the sensitivity of the lake that visitors must obtain a permit, but snorkelling with these harmless, highly photogenic jellyfish is a once-in-a-lifetime experience.
● *By Tasmin Waby*

Festivals & events

Earth Day isn't just another half-hearted observation on Palau. The islands' biological sensitivity, the threat of global warming, and Palauan climate action combine to make this a really significant entry in the calendar. If you're visiting on 22 April 2016, you can get involved in clean-up initiatives, diving and kayaking to collect detritus from the lagoons.

Every 9 July (Constitution Day), Palau celebrates the passing of the world's first nuclear-free constitution. While the biggest celebrations are in Koror, the accompanying festival celebrates the distinctive arts and culture of the entire archipelago.

ONCE THE MOST IMPORTANT STRONGHOLD OF THE LIVONIAN ORDER, THE CRUMBLING MEDIEVAL CASTLE AT CESIS TODAY HOUSES A MUSEUM

BEST IN TRAVEL 2016

Latvia

Hundreds of crumbling castles and manor houses – from medieval to Rococo – hide in Latvia's dense forests of pine

OFF-ROAD | FOOD | ACTIVITIES

Population: **2 million**

Foreign visitors per year: **2.1 million**

Capital: **Rīga**

Languages: **Latvian, Russian**

Major industry: **manufacturing (chemicals, food and drink, wood)**

Unit of currency: **euro (€)**

Cost index: **fish soup €8 (US$8.45), mid-range hotel double room €50 (US$52), tickets to the National Opera €10 (US$10.60), commuter train from Rīga to the beach €1.40 (US$1.50)**

Why go in 2016?

> *Latvia is shining for its silver anniversary*

Celebrating 25 years of freedom from its Soviet fetters, little Latvia is poised to take centre stage after more than two decades of playing catch-up with many of its European brethren. And the title of 'most improved' is rightfully deserved for casting aside the dismal shadow of Communism and resuscitating centuries-old traditions that have long made this Baltic treasure shine.

Hundreds of crumbling castles and manor houses – from medieval to Rococo – hide in the nation's dense forests of pine, and today many of

Life-changing experience

Cast modesty aside and indulge in Latvia's most Latvian tradition, the *pirts* – a hot birch sauna. A traditional *pirts* is run by a sauna master who cares for her naked attendees while performing choreographed branch beatings that draw on ancient pagan traditions. Herbs and wildflowers swish in the air to raise the humidity in the chamber for a series of sweltering 15-minute sessions before you exit the sauna to jump in a nearby body of water (lake, pond or sea). Nibbles and tipples, like smoked fish and beer, are intermixed for good measure, in what is largely the best way to swap the latest gossip with locals.

> *Over the summer solstice, Latvians flock to the countryside for bonfires, beers and plenty of naked frolicking*

these estates have been lavishly transformed into inns and museums. In fact an entire week could be spent in the countryside connecting the stars of this constellation.

Food, too, has come a long way from sweaty pork and potatoes. A fleet of (new) New Nordic chefs are catapulting local flavours to such artisanal heights that they would truly give Copenhagen a run for its money if Michelin were paying them more attention.

And as the country's rural population continues to dwindle, Rīga, the capital, further bolsters its importance throughout both the country and the region, especially after receiving a generous infusion of EU funds during its reign as European Capital of Culture in 2014. Much of the money was earmarked for infrastructure improvements and major renovations to important civic structures like the former KGB headquarters (now a fascinating museum), and the clutch of coveted Art Nouveau façades, of which the city has over 700 – one of the largest collections in the world.

Festivals & events

Held over the summer solstice, **Līgo and Jāņi (23 and 24 June) are the nation's most important days,** collectively celebrated with deep pagan undertones. Latvians flock to the countryside for bonfires, beers, and plenty of naked frolicking.

Locals celebrate their independence on 18 November, known as Proclamation Day, which commemorates the fateful day in 1918 when the nation had its first taste of freedom from Russia. Although Latvia regained its independence from the Soviet Union on 4 May many decades later, 18 November is marked by celebrations today, including a massive parade through the capital during which thousands of people lay flowers at the foot of 'Milda', the Freedom Monument, unveiled on the same day in 1935.

Random facts

▪ It's believed that the Christmas tree originated in Latvia. In 1510 a fraternity of drunken bachelors hauled a pine tree into Rīga's town square, covered it in flowers and set it on fire. A plaque marks the spot where the burning tree once stood.

▪ A Latvian named Arvīds Blūmentāls was the inspiration for Crocodile Dundee. Originally from a town in western Latvia called Dundaga, he moved to Australia after the WWII, where he hunted reptiles and dug for opals.

▪ Technically the Latvian language has no word for 'mountain'; the same word is used for 'hill' and 'mountain'. No wonder, since Latvia's highest point, Gaiziņkalns, is only 312m high.

Most bizarre sight

Gauja National Park may be known as a pine-studded preserve filled with medieval ruins, but it also holds some of the most eccentric relics from the Soviet era. Don't miss the 1200m cement bobsled track built near Sigulda as the training course for the Soviet Olympic team, and check out the top-secret nuclear fallout shelter buried under a convalescence home in Līgatne. The bunker was of high strategic importance during the Cold War and the rooms covered in untouched switchboards and Soviet propaganda will undoubtedly perk the antenna of any Bond enthusiast.

● *By Brandon Presser*

THE MIDSUMMER FESTIVAL IN JŪRMALA PROVIDES THE PERFECT EXCUSE FOR A BEACH BONFIRE

BEST IN
TRAVEL
2016

THE SKYLINE-DOMINATING OPERA HOUSE ATTRACTS
EIGHT MILLION TOURISTS EVERY YEAR – EQUIVALENT
TO OVER A THIRD OF AUSTRALIA'S ENTIRE POPULATION

Australia

Australia does a roaring trade in Unesco World Heritage wilderness areas. What they have in common is a humbling sense of awe at first sight

OFF-ROAD   CULTURE   VALUE

Population: **23.1 million**
Foreign visitors per year: **6.3 million**
Capital: **Canberra**
Language: **English**
Unit of currency: **Australian dollar (A$)**
Major industry: **mining**
Cost index: **cup of coffee A$4 (US$3), hotel double A$100-250 (US$76-190), short taxi ride A$20 (US$15), car hire per day from A$35 (US$27)**

→ ___

Why go in 2016? › *Reefs, forests & indigenous culture*

Unless you're from New Zealand or Papua New Guinea, Australia can seem a long way from anywhere. Getting here usually involves folding yourself into a plane for 24 hours. But with 2016 shaping up as a defining year for several of Australia's key wilderness areas, it'll be 24 hours well spent. In fact, with the weak Australian dollar, *anything* you spend here this year will be value for money. Petrol prices are heading south too: perfect timing for your Great Australian Road Trip.

Environmentally, battle lines are being drawn near the Great Barrier Reef in Queensland, where a string of proposed mining ports will require the dredging and dumping of millions of tonnes of seafloor. In Tasmania, a peace accord between pro- and anti-logging forces has been torn up by the new state government, keen to unlock old-growth forest for export. Now is the time to experience these astounding wilderness areas before compromises are made.

More positively, increasing numbers of Aboriginal land rights claims are being recognised here, including recent claims over Queensland's Fraser Island and a huge tract of South Australia's Eyre Peninsula. Indigenous tourism is booming, with new Aboriginal tour companies such as Ngurrangga Tours in Karratha and Bungoolee Tours in the Kimberley offering authentic cultural experiences. Contemporary Aboriginal art remains an Australian cultural high-water mark, as evidenced by the fab new Godinymayin Yijard Rivers Arts & Culture Centre in Katherine.

Life-changing experiences

Australia does a roaring trade in Unesco World Heritage wilderness areas: the 2300km-long Great Barrier Reef; the blood-red rocks of Uluru and Kata Tjuta; the 15,800 sq km Tasmanian Wilderness Area; the seething jungle of Kakadu National Park... Given the cross-continental distances involved, you mightn't see them all – but what they have in common is a humbling sense of awe at first sight.

What's hot...
Fremantle, Chet Faker, Tasmanian whisky

...What's not
Australian tennis, Tasmanian government forest policy, shark attacks

Current craze

Food vans and small bars. Battling innumerable fast-food joints in Australian cities, the current clog of takeaway food vans – serving everything from burgers to barramundi curry – is constantly expanding. Afterwards, sip a craft beer at the latest alleyway speakeasy around the corner.

Trending topics

Real estate is the national addiction. Australians love talking about it, building it, buying it, looking at it on TV and (most of all) making money selling it. When the GFC jumped up and bit everybody in 2008, world real estate prices tumbled – but not in Australia. A glorious mining boom was in full swing: Australians just kept on buying pricey houses, driving the market skywards. Now – having reached a tipping point where the median house price is more than five times the median annual household income – Australian house prices are among the least affordable on the planet. Will the bubble burst?

A DROVER LOOKS OUT TO THE MOUNT MULLIGAN MOUNTAIN RANGE, QUEENSLAND

MATT MUNRO © LONELY PLANET IMAGES

January's Tour Down Under is Australia's version of the Tour de France, with lycra-clad lads racing around South Australia. Picnic rugs and champagne are viewing essentials.

In the quiet depths of the Tasmanian winter (mid-June), Dark MOFO delivers a seductive programme of installations and performances that will rattle your rusty cage.

Aussie Rules football is high-flying, emotional and a bit weird. Don't miss the Australian Football League Grand Final, played every September or October in Melbourne. Tickets are like gold: watch it in a pub or at someone's backyard barbecue instead.

Random facts

■ Australia is the sixth-largest country in the world (behind Russia, Canada, China, the USA and Brazil).

■ When the British landed in 1788, Australia comprised more than 500 different Aboriginal nations, with distinct languages and territories.

■ Since the inception of the Man Booker Prize for literature in 1969, four Australians have won: Peter Carey (twice), Thomas Keneally, DBC Pierre and Richard Flanagan.

■ Since Europeans arrived in Australia, 27 native mammal, 23 bird and 78 frog species are believed to have become extinct.

Emerging from the haze in the central Australian desert is a kooky roadside installation featuring several large aeroplanes welded together

Most bizarre sight

Emerging from the haze on the far-flung Oodnadatta Track in the central Australian desert is the Mutonia Sculpture Park – a kooky roadside installation featuring several large aeroplanes welded together with their tails buried in the ground to form 'Planehenge'. ● *By Charles Rawlings-Way*

MARKET SQUARE IN THE OLD
TOWN OF WROCŁAW, POLAND

Poland

Wrocław is poised for stardom as a European Capital of Culture, makeovers are adding lustre to lesser-known cities, and wildlife tourism is on the rise

CULTURE | FAMILY | ADVENTURE

Population: **38.5m**
Foreign visitors per year: **15.8m**
Capital: **Warsaw**
Language: **Polish**
Major industries: **mining, agriculture, manufacturing**
Unit of currency: **złoty (zł)**
Cost index: **portion of street food *oscypek*, a smoked sheep's cheese 2zł (US$0.50), bottle of Żywiec beer in a cafe 8zł (US$2), half-day guided bison-spotting walk in Białowieża 240zł (US$61), apartment in Wrocław per night 200zł (US$51)**

Why go in 2016?
> *Cultural capital crowns Poland's rise to the top*

If any country in Europe can boast superpowers, it's Poland. The nation defied a recession that brought the rest of Europe to its knees, and visitor numbers continue to climb. Sceptics said Poland's luck would wane after the country co-hosted the Euro 2012 football championship. Instead, Wrocław is poised for stardom as a European Capital of Culture, makeovers are adding lustre to lesser-known cities, and wildlife tourism is on the rise. Clearly 2016 is the year to put the icing on the cake – or perhaps, the swirl of *śmietana* in the beetroot soup.

Wrocław, the historical capital of Silesia, already had plenty of reasons to preen. Its Old Town Hall, with gothic turrets firing off a custard-coloured exterior, is one of Poland's most beautiful buildings. And among beer gardens and soaring bell towers, Wrocław harbours a show-stopping 114m-long painting, the *Panorama Racławicka*. Highlights of the city's stint as one of 2016's European Capitals of Culture will be an artist-in-residence programme to promote artists across borders and world music days that combine influences across 50 different countries.

Kraków too will sparkle this year for World Youth Day, when the Pope touches down to kick off a calendar of celebrations and activism. In a country nearly 90% Roman Catholic, the turnout in picturesque Kraków is sure to be record-breaking.

And while budget airlines have long spidered their way across Poland, access is even easier with British Airways now flying London to Kraków, Wizz Air opening routes to Szczecin and Katowice, and Finnair launching one to Gdańsk. Any lingering condescension about how well this post-Soviet country is muddling along will vanish as quickly as a shot of tangy *wiśniówka* (cherry vodka).

Life-changing experiences

■ Plummet 135m into the Wieliczka Salt Mine for an unforgettable underground adventure. In this yawning Unesco-listed grotto,

Festivals & events

Unlock Poland's rich Jewish history in late June to early July at Kraków's Jewish Culture Festival.

Witness a tidal wave of optimism and spiritual uplift in Kraków at World Youth Day events from 25–31 July.

Brush up on your bartering skills at St Dominic's Fair in Gdańsk from late July to mid-August.

Gobble dumplings until you pop a button at Kraków's mid-August Pierogi Fair.

Settle in for arthouse screenings at Warsaw's International Film Festival in October.

Hundreds of bison lumber through Białowieża forest – though we'd wager the first one you spot will grace the label on a bottle of Poland's legendary bisongrass vodka, Żubrówka

BEST IN TRAVEL 2016

carvings grace walls and chandeliers drip from ceilings – all of them made out of salt. Other subterranean sights offer a glimpse into some of Poland's most colourful myths. Beneath Kraków's Wawel Hill lies the rumoured lair of a slain dragon, while in the chalk tunnels of Chełm you'll learn of a legendary white bear, now the city's emblem.

■ Hundreds of bison lumber through Białowieża Forest – though we'd wager the first one you spot will grace the label on a bottle of Poland's legendary bisongrass vodka, Żubrówka. Unesco-listed Białowieża is the last remaining expanse of the vast forest that once spread across the European plain. The 141,885-hectare forest (which extends into neighbouring Belarus) is home to around 900 bison, more than half of which are in the Polish reserve. The forest is also prowled by elk, wolves and lynx.

■ Weekenders looking beyond well-loved Warsaw and Kraków are now spoilt for choice. Increasing visitor numbers mean that Łódź, with its 19th-century mansions and cafe-strewn Piotrkowska Street, is abuzz with redevelopment. Meanwhile Szczecin continues to add polish to its Old Town and is now luring golfers to nearby Binowo Park.

Trending topic

Poland's heavy-metal scene elicits headbanging or howls of dismay, depending on whom you ask. Some of Poland's heaviest artists have risen to global acclaim, in particular Behemoth, who loudly protest Poland's religious majority in between bouts of imperious black metal. To some, they are champions of a new, more secular Poland; to many, they're the terror of the nation. Wherever you fall in the debate, you'll never associate Poland with folk dancing again.

Most bizarre sight

Wrocław's gnomes commemorate the 1980s thanks to Orange Alternative movement, an anti-Communist group known for its absurdist style of protest – including dwarf graffiti and gnome-hat demonstrations. Today more than 300 gnome statues wave from street corners and twirl their beards beneath window panes. Gnomes with canes and wheelchairs have been added to the elfin army, to draw attention to the challenges faced by people in Wrocław with disabilities.

● *By Anita Isalska*

EUROPEAN BISON HULK THROUGH BIAŁOWIEŻA FOREST

ANOTHER DAY DRAWS TO
A STUNNING CLOSE AT
PUNTA DEL ESTE

Uruguay

This small country packs a big punch. What it lacks in size, it makes up for in peacefulness, hospitality and personality

OFF-ROAD | CULTURE | FOOD

Population: **3.4 million**
Foreign visitors per year: **2.8 million**
Capital: **Montevideo**
Language: **Spanish**
Major industries: **cattle farming, tourism**
Unit of currency: **Uruguayan peso (UR$)**
Cost index: **glass of beer UR$30 (US$1.16), hotel double in Montevideo UR$1500 (US$58), beef steak in a restaurant UR$300 (US$11.67), car rental per day UR$200 (US$51)**

 8

→ ***Why go in 2016?*** *> Much more than a buffer state*

Squished between South America's two titans, Brazil and Argentina, this small country packs a big punch. What it lacks in size, it makes up for in peacefulness, hospitality and personality. While its two boisterous neighbours lurch from one crisis to the next, Uruguay stands out as a haven of political stability, good governance and prosperity – it's not dubbed 'the Switzerland of America' for nothing. Uruguayans may seem shy and low-key, but they pride themselves on having constructed one of the continent's most progressive societies – without civil conflict.

After two centuries living in the shadow of its neighbours, Uruguay is now eager to promote its identity and assets as more than just a side trip from nearby Buenos Aires. In 2016, it's expected that the number of foreign visitors will reach the 3 million mark. But what is it that these holidaymakers come for?

Take Montevideo, which must be the safest capital in South America. When it comes to quality of life, Montevideo is unrivalled on the continent. It's small enough to get around, but big enough to have some great architecture and a superb restaurant scene. The beach-lined seafront is easily navigated by bike, as is the Old Town, with its array of grand 19th-century neoclassical buildings.

An hour's drive away lies *gaucho* (cowboy) country. Here, undulating pampas are dotted with working *estancias* (cattle ranches), many of which serve as guesthouses. For great nightlife and sexy beaches, head to Punta del Este, a modern resort city on the Atlantic coast full of beautiful people. But if you're weary of high-rise buildings and cocktail bars, venture further east to Cabo Polonio and Punta del Diablo. These fabulously remote fishing-surfing villages peppered with colourful wooden cabins are seeing an influx of visitors, drawn by the bohemian vibes, empty beaches, shifting sand dunes, seal colonies and superb waves. Need some cultural sustenance? The gorgeous town of Colonia del Sacramento delivers the perfect blend of authenticity and tourism development. A Unesco World Heritage site, this ancient Portuguese stronghold, with its cobblestoned alleyways, postcolonial ruins, art galleries and elegant B&Bs, has enough to keep visitors happy for days.

Life-changing experience

Uruguayans are the masters of the *asado* barbecue (but don't tell Argentines and Brazilians!). One of the best and most atmospheric places to sample Uruguayan beef is the Mercado del Puerto in Montevideo. This 19th-century wrought-iron market hall shelters a gaggle of steakhouses. Pull up a stool at any of the *parrillas* (steakhouses) and watch the weighty slabs of meat being cooked over hot coals on a grill, then sink your teeth into a tasty *morcilla* (blood sausage) – memorable! Saturday lunchtime, when the market is crammed with locals, is the best time to visit.

Random facts

■ Uruguayans consume even more maté (a strong green tea) than Argentines and Paraguayans – which is saying a lot.
■ The 29th of each month is Gnocchi Day, when most restaurants serve gnocchi. This tradition dates back to tough economic times when these potato dumplings were the only thing people could afford to cook at the end of the month.
■ Marijuana is produced and sold legally. Home growers are allowed to keep up to six cannabis plants per household.

© JEAN-BERNARD CARILLET

Top 10 Countries ● ● ●

BEST IN TRAVEL 2016

40

Most bizarre sight

In Punta del Este, you can't miss *La Mano de Punta del Este* (The Hand). This quirky iron and cement sculpture by Chilean artist Mario Irarrázabal was created for an art contest in 1982 and has been a 'Punta' fixture ever since. It's unsurprisingly selfie-friendly – thousands of visitors pose in front of its large digits, with the beach in the background.

● *By Jean-Bernard Carillet*

These fabulously remote fishing-surfing villages peppered with colourful wooden cabins are seeing an influx of visitors, drawn by the bohemian vibes, empty beaches, shifting sand dunes, seal colonies and superb waves

INDULGE IN A BARBECUED MEAT FEAST AT A URUGUAYAN STEAKHOUSE IN MERCADO DEL PUERTO

DYED SEALSKIN
LEATHER IS USED
MAKE GREENLAND'S
TRADITIONAL COSTUME

BEST IN
TRAVEL
2016

Greenland

> Come to see the midnight sun glowing on the glaciers, sail among breaching whales, ride across the tundra on a dogsled, watch the Northern Lights

ACTIVITIES	ADVENTURE	OFF-ROAD

Population: **57,728**

Foreign visitors per year: **70,000**

Capital: **Nuuk**

Languages: **Greenlandic, Danish**

Major industries: **fishing, mining**

Unit of currency: **Danish kroner (Dkr)**

Cost index: **hotel room Dkr1275 krone (US$180), dinner at Nipisa, Nuuk's finest restaurant Dkr295 (US$42), two-hour dogsled ride, Dkr895 (US$125), round-trip flight from Kangerlussuaq to the Ilulissat Icefjord Dkr4009 (US$425)**

Why go in 2016?
> *As the earth gets hotter, so does Arctic travel*

Our world is ever warmer, ever more crowded, and ever more plugged-in. So there's something wildly refreshing about a place that's about 80% ice covered, boasts the world's lowest population density, and has cellular coverage so poor that many rely on satellite phones. Come to see the midnight sun on the glaciers, sail among breaching whales, ride across the tundra on a dogsled, watch the Northern Lights dance across the ice sheet.

In March 2016 Greenland (technically a territory of Denmark rather than an independent country, although one with a great deal of autonomy) will

THE TINY FISHING HAMLET OF OQAATSUT
IS HOME TO AROUND 50 GREENLANDERS

host the Arctic Winter Games, the largest event of its kind ever. Competitions range from snowshoeing to native games like pole-pushing (think reverse tug-of-war with a tree trunk). There will also be a cultural festival with song, dance and food. If you're going to visit Greenland, this is the time to go. Luckily for you, it is easier than ever to access. It's a quick four-hour flight from Copenhagen to Kangerlussuaq, Greenland's main airport. And now there are also seasonal flights to Nuuk from Reykjavík in Iceland.

Life-changing experiences

■ Witness icebergs the size of the Empire State Building calving in the Ilulissat Icefjord, home to the northern hemisphere's most productive glacier. The town of Ilulissat, next to the glacier, is known as the 'iceberg capital of the world', and offers a huge number of iceberg-watching adventures. Kayak through the fjord's navy blue waters, soar above the glacier in a fixed-wing plane, or hike along the icy cliffs with a pair of crampons strapped to your shoes.

■ From September to April, Greenland becomes one of the world's prime places to see the aurora borealis, nature's own laser light show. Though you can see the eerie green sine waves from anywhere in the country, for a true once-in-a-lifetime

Festivals & events

After more than a month of endless polar night, Greenlanders celebrate the Return of the Sun in mid-January. Villages throw their own celebrations with cake, coffee and singing as the sun cracks the horizon.

21st June is both the longest day of the year and Greenland's National Day. Expect flag waving, folk dancing, and plenty of *kaffemik*, the beloved Greenlandic tradition of drinking coffee, eating cake, and catching up on the gossip.

On 13 December, children honour St Lucia, a popular Scandinavian saint, with candlelit processions and singing.

Greenlanders get double the party on New Year's Eve, celebrating the Danish New Year on Danish time at 8pm, then local New Year four hours later.

There are no roads between towns and settlements in Greenland. Locals and visitors must travel by plane, boat, snowmobile or sled

experience join a dogsledding expedition to the interior, where you can pitch a tent on the ice sheet and watch the sky in delicious solitude.

Current craze

Eating local. Yeah, yeah, so calling yourself a locavore is trendy everywhere from Peoria to Little Whinging these days. But Greenland is an Arctic island with little agriculture and no ground transportation. So cooking and eating local here is *hardcore*. A new generation of young chefs, some of whom have trained abroad in Denmark or elsewhere, are taking on the challenge and making meals with the delicious, albeit limited, local ingredients. Think juniper-poached musk-ox fillets, razorbill with crowberries, kelp salad studded with reindeer bacon, bellflower *gelée* atop local honey ice cream.

Trending topic

Though Greenland sits atop substantial uranium deposits, the mining of radioactive materials was illegal for a quarter century. Then, in 2013, uranium mining was approved by the government in a close and hotly debated vote. Now the country must decide whether to move forward. Some decry the environmental hazards and potential destruction of Greenland's way of life, while others say the mining of uranium and other substances is the key to Greenland's financial woes.

Random facts

- The iceberg that took down the *Titanic* most likely came from Ilulissat Icefjord in western Greenland, where it began as a snowflake some 15,000 years earlier.
- Greenland's first brewery invented 'ice beer' – beer brewed with water from melted icebergs.
- There are no roads between towns and settlements in Greenland. Locals and visitors must travel by plane, boat, snowmobile or sled.

● *By Emily Matchar*

COME TO FIJI
TO SCUBA DIVE
AMONG ITS
KALEIDOSCOPIC
SOFT CORALS

BEST IN
TRAVEL
2016

Fiji

Blessed by natural beauty and the kind of climate that makes clothes seem a tiresome necessity, today there is a palpable and unprecedented vitality and confidence to Fiji

ACTIVITIES   FAMILY   OFF-ROAD

Population: **881,065**
Foreign visitors per year: **659,112**
Capital: **Suva**
Languages: **Fijian, English, Fiji Hindi**
Major industries: **tourism, sugar, agriculture**
Unit of currency: **Fiji dollar (FJ$)**
Cost index: **cup of coffee FJ$5 (US$2.50), glass of beer FJ$5 (US$2.50), 5km taxi ride FJ$6.50 (US$3.25), reef snorkelling FJ$60 (US$30), scenic flight per person FJ$400 (US$200)**

10

Why go in 2016? › *Fiji's got its groove back*

After an uncertain decade following the coup of Commodore 'Frank' Bainimarama in 2006, and the constitutional crisis of 2009, Fiji has reverted to its peaceful and pleasure-loving self. In late 2014, Bainimarama finally made good on his promise to hold democratic elections, winning the prime ministership and restoring something of constitutional normality (albeit to a situation he had played an important part in creating).

The 2016 upgrade of the Nadi International Airport should increase capacity and make the transition to paradise a little smoother. Fiji's

Festivals & events

For New Year's Eve (31 December), party town Suva will be buzzing at the harbour-front Albert Park for a 12-hour street party featuring live music, dancing, drumming and fireworks. Sure, New Year's happens everywhere, but it happens in Fiji first.

Thanks to the country's substantial Indian population, Diwali – the Hindu Festival of Light – brings colourful candlelit celebrations to Fiji on 30 October.

The Corona Uprising Festival of Music, Dance and Lights at the Uprising Beach Resort continues the party in November with music, dance performances and beachfront bonfires.

international carrier, Fiji Airways, thinks your Fiji experience should begin as soon as you get on board a flight. Those smiles from the cabin crew are just the beginning.

Always blessed by natural beauty and the kind of climate that makes clothes seem a tiresome necessity, today there is a palpable and unprecedented vitality and confidence to Fiji. Whether your bent is idling in a resort, putting your body on the line sampling the latest extreme sport, or the more classic island delights of diving, sailing and angling, 2016 will the year to soak up all Fiji has to offer.

Life-changing experiences

■ It's hard to visit Fiji without being serenaded by warm and welcoming singers brandishing guitars or ukuleles. There will be singing at the airport, at your hotel, and even on local buses. But for a real peek into this very traditional culture's everyday life, get to a village church on a Sunday. Dress modestly (ask locals for advice on what's appropriate) and have your spirits raised by the voices of a community singing traditional songs in harmony.

■ Floating in the turquoise waters of the Mamanuca islands is a two-storey pizzeria and bar servicing surfers, divers, sailors and holidaymakers. Swim up and order your a wood-fired margherita, lounge on a day bed listening to the surround-sound music, and then 'cannonball' back into the spectacular ocean below. Kids are catered for (though did we mention it is completely surrounded by sea?) and prices for the day are all-inclusive. Cloud 9 is a 40-minute speedboat ride from Viti Levu, or a short hop from Musket Cove Island Resort.

■ Nothing will bring out your inner Attenborough like diving Fiji's Somosomo Strait off the garden island of Taveuni. Crowned the 'soft coral capital of the world', Rainbow Reef is famous for its marine life, and the luminescent Great White Wall, a vertical drop-off reached by a tubular swim-through, is covered in soft white coral that looks like glimmering snow. The islands of Vanua Levu and Taveuni also boast bird watching and forest hiking for the nature-loving land lubber.

> **It's hard to visit Fiji without being serenaded by warm and welcoming singers brandishing guitars or ukuleles**

Current craze

Just when you thought the human talent for frivolous invention had exhausted all potential for new 'sports', along comes flyboarding. Essentially a jet-propelled, hand-controlled hoverboard, the flyboard allows you to skim above the waves, shoot high into the air, plunge into the swell, then do it all again! Try it at Bounty Island.

Trending topic

Music from the African New World has taken root on the Fijian islands. What started in imitation of the original US and Jamaican styles has evolved into distinctive local variants: artists such as E.3 & Cracker (hip hop), 1stribe (reggae) and Kula Kei Uluivuya or KKU (pop) still pay homage to their musical roots, but reflect the experiences of Polynesians today.

Most bizarre sight

Vilavilairevo (fire-walking) was originally performed only by the Sawau tribe of Beqa, an island off Viti Levu's southern coast, but now you'll probably catch a performance anywhere in Fiji. Traditionally, strict taboos dictated the men's behaviour leading up to the ceremony and it was believed adherence to these protected them from burns.

● *By Tasmin Waby*

PICTURE PERFECT: FIJI'S REMOTE ISLANDS PROMISE A TROPICAL GETAWAY LIKE NO OTHER

© JONGCHEOL PARK/EYEEM/GETTY IMAGES

Lonely Planet's
Top 10
Regions

TROYANA © GETTY IMAGES

ROMANIAN FARMERS
TRUNDLE THROUGH
THE COUNTRYSIDE

Transylvania, Romania

When a breeze rattles the pastel-coloured wooden shutters and scarlet-clad Roma villagers march through the fields, this region casts a powerful spell

VALUE   CULTURE   ADVENTURE

Population: **7.2m**
Foreign visitors per year: **1.5m**
Main city: **Cluj-Napoca**
Languages: **Romanian, Hungarian**
Major industries: **agriculture, minerals, automotive, electronics**
Unit of currency: **Romanian leu (plural lei)**
Cost index: **cabbage rolls with polenta and cream 15 lei (US$4), four-hour ski pass in Poiana Braşov 95 lei (US$23), double room in a guest-house 150 lei (US$36)**

Why go in 2016?
> *Mountain thrills and edgy art in Vlad's former home*

Drive a stake into the heart of those Transylvanian stereotypes. Yes, this region of Romania has all the moody castles and fog-draped mountains you can wave a crucifix at. But visit Transylvania today and you're just as likely to sashay through a wickedly inventive art gallery, spy on bears, or ski the Carpathian Mountains.

Transylvania is experiencing a renaissance. Cluj-Napoca was dubbed an art city of the future by Phaidon, and Braşov is attracting as many nightlife lovers as vampire hunters. Horses and carts still rattle through the countryside,

A WINTRY OUTLOOK OVER THE COMMUNE OF BRAN, OVERLOOKED BY THE CARPATHIAN MOUNTAINS

GIUSEPPERIZZO @ GETTY IMAGES/FLICKR RF

but they'll soon share the roads with Uber cabs, as the app-based transport network sets up a new office in Bucharest. Meanwhile Transylvanian Airbnb listings are slowly amassing, excellent news for fans of social accommodation.

Beyond the towns, all eyes are on Transylvania's real fang-toothed predators: wolves, lynx and the majority of Romania's 6000-strong bear population. With the recent reintroduction of bison to the Carpathian Mountains, opportunities for wildlife watching are sure to become even richer. Controversially the government still issues hunting permits for animals perceived as a threat, and there's been criticism of building sites encroaching on natural spaces. But attitudes are changing in this country once infamous for bear-baiting. Wildlife sanctuaries such as Libearty are thriving, while eco-conscious operators such as Ibis and Carpathian Nature Tours ply the mountains. At long last Transylvania's natural riches are taking centre stage.

Life-changing experiences

■ There's reinvention in the air in Cluj-Napoca, which is feted as one of Europe's emerging art hubs. The acclaim is largely thanks to the Fabrica de Pensule (Paintbrush Factory), an art collective with six mini-galleries. But the buzz is helped in no small part by Cluj's quirky museums and nightlife, which deftly marries cellar boozeries with a handful of achingly trendy indie bars.

■ Excellent snow for a small price tag is every skier's dream. Best of all, in Transylvania there's no need to hole up in a remote ski resort. Poiana Braşov is only half an hour from Braşov city, and Păltiniş, one of Romania's highest resorts at 1440m, is less than an hour from Sibiu.

■ Cutting-edge art and a taste for the piste haven't eclipsed the rural Romania of your imagination. Fortified churches sprout across Transylvania, with some of the best in Biertan and Viscri. When a breeze rattles the pastel-coloured wooden shutters and scarlet-clad Roma villagers march through the fields, this region casts a powerful spell.

■ Still hoping for a glimpse of Dracula? Look hard amid the 'Count Drankula' souvenir T-shirts and forget what you learned from Bram Stoker (whose 19th-century novel only takes loose inspiration from Transylvania). For some, the historical Vlad Dracul – 'Dragon' to his friends, 'Impaler' to his impalees – is a national hero for seeing off Ottoman invaders through a range of grisly tactics. Hardcore Vlad fans will want to venture to his strategic Poenari Citadel in neighbouring Wallachia, but the Transylvanian Vlad trail focuses on delightfully colourful Sighişoara, his birthplace.

Festivals & events

Join Cluj's cinema fanatics at the Transylvania International Film Festival in late May/early June.

Beware the full moon at the late July Luna Plina Horror Film Festival in Biertan.

Grab a drinking horn and your finest wimple at the Sighişoara Medieval Festival on the last weekend in July.

Welcome the woolly ones home at Transylvania's shepherd festivals in September, such as the Shepherds' Fall Festival in Poiana Sibiului.

Random facts

■ Don't surprised if your nose lengthens on Sibiu's iron bridge. The 1859 span is known as 'Liars' Bridge', thanks to haggling market sellers and (local legends claim) sweethearts declaring their virginity to one another.

■ The path from Buckingham Palace to Braşov might not seem immediately apparent, but Prince Charles supports a number of conservation projects in Transylvania. The UK royal has even planted a wildflower meadow at England's Highgrove Gardens to remind him of the Transylvanian countryside.

Most bizarre sight

With gold-embossed murals and a multi-coloured tiled roof, Târgu Mureş' Palace of Culture is one of the region's most bewilderingly beautiful sights.

Wonders increase inside, especially in the flashy Hall of Mirrors (Sala Oglinzi). Here local folklore is lovingly embossed in stained glass, from fairy tales to Satanic ravishment. Shield the kids' eyes for this one.

Regional flavours

Romanian *sarmale*, a cabbage leaf roll of seasoned meat, and *mămăligă*, cornmeal porridge, often studded with sheep's cheese and bacon, perpetually lavish plates. But in Székely Land, where ethnic Hungarians outnumber Romanians, there's an extra sprinkling of paprika. With Hungarian goulash, Romanian *papanaşi* (curd-stuffed donuts) and banquets of grilled meat, there are plenty of reasons to raise a glass of *ţuică*, the local firewater, to the chef.

● *By Anita Isalska*

BEST IN
TRAVEL
2016

THE FISHING HAMLET OF ARNASTAPI
ATTRACTS HIKERS TO ITS BEACHES AND
NEARBY LAVA FIELDS IN SUMMER

West Iceland

This vast and varied region captures all the best of Iceland's off-the-charts wildlife and nature: cloud-shrouded glaciers, rugged lava fields, gushing waterfalls and lush green fields

ADVENTURE | ACTIVITIES | OFF-ROAD

Population: **21,630**
Main town: **Borgarnes**
Languages: **Icelandic, English**
Major industries: **fishing, agriculture**
Unit of currency: **Icelandic króna (Ikr)**
Cost index: **glass of beer Ikr500-700 (US$4-5); guesthouse double room with bathroom Ikr22,000 (US$160); whale-watching tour Ikr850 (US$63); glacier tour Ikr9000-22,000 (US$65-160)**

Why go in 2016? > *Top adventures in a land of raw beauty*

West Iceland may be just a short two-hour drive from the capital of Iceland (natty little Reykjavík), but it's remained largely off tourists' radars. This vast and varied region captures all the best of Iceland's off-the-charts wildlife and nature: cloud-shrouded glaciers, rugged lava fields crisscrossed by gigantic lava tubes, gushing waterfalls, and lush green fields perfect for horse riding. Its 90km-long Snæfellsnes Peninsula and Snæfellsjökull National Park are crowned by the glistening ice cap Snæfellsjökull, immortalised in Jules Verne's *Journey to the Centre of the Earth.* Plus whales, seals, puffins and dozens of other seabirds cavort off the coast.

Festivals & events

Þorrablót, a Viking midwinter feast (late January to mid/late February), is marked with stomach-churning treats such as *hákarl* (fermented shark), *svið* (singed sheep's head) and *hrútspungar* (rams' testicles). All accompanied by shots of *Brennivín* (a potent schnapps nicknamed 'black death'). Hungry?

In late June, Brákarhátíð festival in Borgarnes honours Þorgerður Brák, the heroine from the medieval Egil's Saga who saved Egil from his shape-shifting father and then swam to her death (the father fatally beans her with a rock). Expect town decorations, parades, a concert and a lively, offshore, mud football match.

The Northern Lights, or aurora borealis, are a colourful, dancing light show caused by charged particles from solar flares colliding with the earth's atmosphere. The best months for viewing are October to April, with peak visibility from December to February.

MAKE FRIENDS WITH WILD HORSES ON SNAEFELLSNESS PENINSULA

As West Iceland's tourism takes off, the question is how to expand the tourist infrastructure while preserving the region's pristine beauty

While Iceland has been seeing tourism growth figures in the double digits (24% in 2014 alone!) and it's become a hot, hot destination (no pun intended), the infrastructure is only now starting to catch up with the demand, with new guesthouses and cafes popping up. In 2016 we can expect the west to finally get the international fanfare it deserves since Into the Glacier, its new man-made ice cave in the Langjökull glacier, is now open to the public and drawing visitors to the blossoming region – get there before the hordes!

Life-changing experiences

West Iceland throws down the gauntlet when choosing your own adventure. What would you

BEST IN
TRAVEL
2016

Top 10 Regions

rather do: explore the new ice cave at Langjökull, climb the glacier that inspired Jules Verne at Snæfellsjökull National Park, scope out puffin colonies or watch breaching whales off the Snæfellsnes Peninsula? Or perhaps you'd prefer to head inland to Hallmundarhraun, an enormous lava field, to explore the country's largest lava tube at Viðgelmir? The choice is yours.

Current craze

West Iceland's popping up on screens from Hollywood to HBO. Look for Ben Stiller skateboarding past West Iceland's Kirkjufell (Iceland's most photographed mountain) in *The Secret Life of Walter Mitty.* Or spot local flora and fauna (particularly an Icelandic goat from this area who gets eaten by a dragon) in TV series *Game of Thrones.*

Trending topic

As West Iceland's tourism takes off, the question of the day is how to expand the tourist infrastructure while preserving the region's pristine beauty. Establishments like farm-guesthouse-artist residency Fljótstunga try to guide visitors to nearby lava tubes while following ecologically and culturally sensitive practices.

Most bizarre sight

The farmstead at Bjarnarhöfn is the region's leading producer of *hákarl* (fermented shark meat), a traditional (and pungent) Icelandic dish. Greenland shark, which is used to make *hákarl*, is poisonous if eaten fresh, so fermentation neutralises the toxin. Bjarnarhöfn's wee museum has exhibits on the history of this culinary curiosity. A word of warning, take pity on the Greenland shark: it is classified as Near Threatened on the IUCN Red List.

Defining difference

West Iceland stands apart for its rich cultural heritage. It has the densest concentration in Iceland of remaining Viking sites. Borgarnes' must-see Settlement Centre offers fascinating insights into the history of Icelandic settlement and the saga era, and recounts the amazing (no hyperbole) adventures of Egil Skallagrímsson (the man behind *Egil's Saga)* and his family, with cairns throughout the area marking the original sites of the action. Inland, Reykholt was home to one of the most important medieval chieftains and scholars, Snorri Sturluson (also killed there), who wrote much of the saga-era history. The Dalir area, a scenic corridor of rolling fields and craggy river-carved buttes, was the setting for the *Laxdæla Saga,* one of the most popular of the Icelandic sagas, while the farm Eiríksstaðir is said to have been home to Erik the Red, father of Leifur Eiríksson, the first European to visit America.

● *By Alexis Averbuck*

Top 10 Regions

BEST IN
TRAVEL
2016

Valle de Viñales, Cuba

Hire a guide to take you hiking, horse riding or cycling through the tobacco fields and mogotes, and enjoy the stunning views across the valleys

ACTIVITIES	CULTURE	FOOD

Population: **27,000**
Main town: **Viñales**
Language: **Spanish**
Major industry: **agriculture, mainly tobacco**
Unit of currency: **Cuban convertible peso (CUC), linked to US$ 1:1, and Cuban peso**
Cost index: **local beer 1 CUC (US$1), room in *casa particular* for one night 25-30 CUC (US$25-30), evening meal in casa 7-10 CUC (US$7-10), very slow internet access 8-10 CUC per hour (US$8-10)**

3

Why go in 2016? > Traditional Cuba at its best

After more than 50 years out in the cold, Cuba's relationship with the US is finally thawing and this Caribbean nation finds itself on the brink of change. Havana may have plenty to offer in terms of architecture, history, music, museums and galleries, but once you've seen the vintage cadillacs, posed with Che Guevara in the Plaza de la Revolución and strolled along the Malecón, then it's time for a taste of the slower pace of life known to many Cubans. For this, head west to the agricultural centre of Valle de Viñales, approximately two hours' drive from the capital.

The wonderful thing about the main town of Viñales is that not only can you relax in a rocking chair on the porch of your *casa particular* (homestay) and watch the oxen and ploughs trundle by, you can also get involved in all kinds of activities in the Unesco-registered landscape. Hire a guide to take you hiking, horse riding or cycling through the tobacco fields and *mogotes* (rock formations), and enjoy the stunning views across the valleys. End with a refreshing swim in a cave, before heading straight back to that rocking chair. Settle down with a cold beer in hand and the sound of live *son* music drifting from one of the bars before indulging in a meal at the *casa* – most *casa* hosts take the quality of their home-cooked dinners very seriously, and you can expect options such as succulent roast chicken or grilled lobster, served with traditional dishes including black bean rice and plantain.

When you're ready for a change of scenery, drive about 60km northwest to Cayo Jutías. This long white-sand beach, reached via a causeway through mangroves, is a great day trip from Viñales. There's very little development here – no hotels and only a couple of restaurants – and, as in Viñales, you can choose between activities (such as snorkelling and kayaking), or lying back and doing absolutely nothing.

TOBACCO CROPS FILL THE VALLEY IN VINALES. BEYOND THEM, LIMESTONE MOGOTES DARE CLIMBERS TO TEST THEIR METTLE

> *In all that wonderful rolling scenery, one peculiar thing a visitor can look out for is a traffic jam made up of oxen and ploughs and horses and carts, with cigar-chewing farmers at the helm*

Festivals & events

The 18th Festival Habanos in February is mainly a trade event, but tobacco aficionados can go along. It includes visits to tobacco plantations and cigar factories near Viñales.

Pinar del Río, the capital of the province that includes Valle de Viñales, holds Carnaval every July. Join in with the drinking and dancing at this large street party.

The biennial International Ballet Festival of Havana is held in October/ November at various venues in Havana, where dance troupes from around the world perform alongside the Ballet Nacional de Cuba.

Even with the prospect of a tourist boom thanks to improved relations with the US, Viñales is likely to retain its traditional charm and slow pace of life. Combined with Havana, it makes the perfect combination for a two-centre trip giving contrasting experiences of Cuba, ideal for US citizens who may now find this fascinating country more accessible to them.

Life-changing experiences

The limestone *mogotes* in Valle de Viñales reach up to 300m high and offer superb opportunities for experienced climbers, with many limestone overhangs and tufa columns. For a more down-to-earth experience, visit a tobacco plantation, roll your own cigar, head back to that rocking chair and resume doing nothing.

Trending topic

Part of the proposed changes in US Cuban relations involves providing software and hardware that will allow improvements to telecommunications across Cuba. This could mean speedier internet access for all, instead of the current expensive and very slow dial-up system that occasionally connects the lucky few tourists with home.

Most bizarre sight

In all that wonderful rolling scenery, one peculiar thing a visitor can look out for is a traffic jam made up of oxen and ploughs and horses and carts, with cigar-chewing farmers (*guajiro*) at the helm.

Defining difference

The African slaves working on the tobacco plantations of Valle de Viñales along with the Spanish conquerors and local people made a massive contribution to creating Cuba's incredible multi-ethnic society. This, along with its unique landscape, makes the valley an area of great cultural significance. ● *By Claire Naylor*

MONTE LUSSARI IN FRIULI VENEZIA
GIULIA IS A WINTER SKI RESORT, BUT
COME IN SUMMER FOR BREATHTAKING
VIEWS FROM ITS CABLE-CAR

BEST IN
TRAVEL
2016

Friuli's wine regions, Italy

From simple farmhouse tables to elegant fine-dining rooms and vertical tastings among the vines, cellar doors are not a tourist attraction: breaking bread and talking terroir is a way of life here

FOOD | CULTURE | OFF-ROAD

Population: **1.22 million (in the whole Friuli Venezia Giulia region)**
Main towns: **Udine and Trieste**
Languages: **Italian, Slovenian, Friulian**
Major industries: **agriculture, shipping**
Unit of currency: **euro (€)**
Cost index: **bottle of wine €10 (US$11), espresso €1 (US$1.10), B&B double room €120 (US$130), daily car hire €35 (US$40)**

Why go in 2016? > *This is Italy, but not as you know it*

The name 'Friuli' has been popping up on smart wine lists around the world these past few years and a handful of boundary-pushing Friulian winemakers have become unlikely cult figures among wine cognoscenti far beyond Italy. While many fans might be content to sniff, swirl and swallow their fine aromatic whites, bold tangy reds and blow-your-mind natural 'oranges' at home, there's a growing number who come to Friuli to experience for themselves the region's rustic wine routes.

The word may be out, but this is still a very little visited destination, even by other Italians. From simple farmhouse tables where the latest vintage comes only by the jug, to elegant fine-dining rooms and vertical tastings among the vines, cellar doors are not a tourist attraction: breaking bread and talking terroir is a way of life.

Several certified growing regions ('DOCs') form a checkerboard between the cities of Udine, Gorizia and Trieste, with the highly respected Collio, Colli Orientali and the wildcard Carso only around an hour's drive apart. In fact, the entire region is far from large, but its many micro-climates mean there's variety to be had both for the palate and in an ever-shifting landscape of rolling hills, plains and no-so-distant Alps.

Life-changing experience

Drive up into the rocky Carso region and hit the winding back roads during spring and it won't be long before you spot your first red wooden arrow adorned with a tree branch. Following the *frasca* is a culinary treasure hunt that's been going on for centuries, with *osmize*, pop-up cellar doors, the prize at the end of the trail. Here winemakers welcome you into their courtyards and barns to sample the Carso's smoky, pear-scented Vitovska and deep violet-tinted Terrano. And because this is Friuli, a plate of cured ham and cheese is never far away.

Current craze

Friuli doesn't just do indigenous grapes – it's also a producer of some increasingly classy Sauvignons. So classy that in 2015, the Concours

Festivals & events

San Daniele's cured ham is Friuli's most widely loved export besides wine; the medieval streets of this hill-top town host Aria di Friuli Venezia Giulia, in what might be the world's biggest celebration of porky products, at the end of June.

Udine welcomes autumn with Friuli DOC in mid-September, another gut-busting food and wine festival devoted to certified local products, including ham, cheese, wine and grappa.

Border town Gorizia celebrates the culinary culture of its neighbours in a four-day feeding frenzy, Gusti di Frontiera, held at the end of September.

> *Winemakers welcome you into their courtyards to sample the Carso's smoky, pear-scented Vitovska and deep violet-tinted Terrano*

CRISPY *FRICO*, MADE FROM FRIULI'S MONTASIO CHEESE, IS A LOCAL DELICACY

Mondial du Sauvignon competition decamped to Friuli, its first ever foray outside France. With the French wine police now paying its respects to Friulian Sauvignon, the rest of the world can't be far behind.

Defining difference

Nestled up in Italy's far northeast, Friuli Venezia Giulia has been Roman, Lombard, Venetian and Austro-Hungarian, with large slivers of the east still part of Slovenia until a hundred years ago. Its cities are, as you might imagine with that pedigree, cosmopolitan and cultural, boasting Tiepolo-ceilinged cathedrals and Habsburg grace and glamour. That said, the Friulani, known for both their stoic reserve and party-hard ways, maintain a close connection with the land.

Local lingo

Up in the Carso, above Trieste, the street signs and locals' names reveal Slovenian origins, and this is still the first language of many of the winemakers. Further north, in Udine and the Collio, you'll often spot Friulian on signs and hear older locals greet each other with a hearty '*bundi!*'.

Regional flavours

Friuli's oft-shifting borders are reflected in its kitchens. Local ravioli, called *cjalsons*, are stuffed with spiced caramelised onions and potatoes or beetroot and smoked ricotta. The local Montasio cheese is the base for the ubiquitous *frico*, that comes either crispy fried or in a soft potato pancake. Local prosciutto, too, is a staple while richly sauced meat dishes often feature rabbit and deer. Ask for a restaurant recommendation from someone in Udine and you'll inevitably be steered towards a place out in the countryside, where these bold-flavoured dishes are served in a rustic setting. ● *By Donna Wheeler*

BEST IN
TRAVEL
2016

**BOAT SHEDS ON THE SHORE
OF WAIHEKE ISLAND AT DUSK**

Waiheke Island, New Zealand

A mere 35-minute ferry ride from downtown Auckland sits an island utopia of secret coves, beautiful beaches, rolling vineyards, luxury lodges and bohemian sensibilities

| FOOD | EVENTS | FAMILY |

Population: **8800**
Foreign visitors per year: **1.1 million**
Language: **English**
Unit of currency: **NZ dollar (NZ$)**
Major industries: **tourism, wine, art**
Cost index: **return ferry ticket from Auckland NZ$36 (US$26), cheese board at Mudbrick Vineyard & Restaurant NZ$35 (US$26), bottle of Obsidian Reserve Syrah NZ$63 (US$46.75), room at the Oyster Inn NZ$199-450 (US$148-334)**

ROBIN BUSH © GETTY IMAGES

5

Why go 2016? > Playground of the Gods

Nestled in the Hauraki Gulf and shouldering the impressive dormant island volcano Rangitoto, a mere 35-minute ferry ride from downtown Auckland sits an island utopia of secret coves, beautiful beaches, rolling vineyards, luxury lodges and bohemian sensibilities. Waiheke Island, New Zealand's third-most densely populated island, is affectionately known as the 'Island of Wine' and home to over 30 wineries and some of the best boutique cellar door experiences New Zealand has to offer. Many wineries boast views of the spectacular Auckland skyline, and you can quaff a Syrah (Shiraz) or rosé, bask in brilliant sunshine, taste local produce and discover the meaning of 'Waiheke time'. Dionysus would approve.

Waiheke's bohemian and hippie past is not far from the surface and the island continues to have a thriving artistic community where over a hundred working artists ply their trades in disciplines such as sculpture, glass blowing, painting and woodwork. Waiheke is an outdoor enthusiast's playground, where mountain biking, sea kayaking and sailing can all be indulged. The island is an electric, heady mix set against a Buddha Bar soundtrack: fast yet slow all at the same time – there's nowhere else on earth quite like it. The secret is out and in 2016 Waiheke Island is welcoming the world to sample from its abundant offerings and inviting all visitors to fall under its spell.

Life-changing experiences

Book a bach. That's what the locals do. A 'bach' is a holiday house that can be used for short-term rental and it's the perfect base from which to explore the island's variety of offerings. And there are plenty of baches – over 450 across the island, bookable online.

On waking to the singing chirp of the cicadas in summer, take a stroll or scooter to Palm Beach for an early morning swim in the cove's shallow, sheltered waters. Then it's off to Wild on Waiheke to sample a beer float before challenging your party to take on archery in the vines. Ride the flying fox zipline across native forest at Eco Zip Adventures before knocking on a few cellar doors such as Mudbrick or Cable Bay to sample the nectar of the island. Finish your evening mingling with locals at the Oyster Inn, where a curated offering of craft beers and local vintages are offered alongside a menu brimming with local produce and fresh oysters. Sleep. Wake. Repeat.

Regional flavours

Waiheke Island's boutique wineries and their accompanying cellar doors and restaurants are the most accessible in New Zealand; a 35-minute journey from Auckland and you'll find yourself sampling your first Syrah. 'The Island of Wine' is best known for its award-winning Syrah, but varietals such as Montepulciano, Pinot Gris, Tempranillo and Viognier can be found among

GRAPEVINES LINE THE HILLSIDE
BY MAN O' WAR BAY ROAD

the island's 30-plus vineyards. With cellar doors offering everything from simple tastings to five-star restaurant experiences, Waiheke has options for all palates and budgets. Many tour companies offer day trips from Auckland that take in a minimum of three cellar doors or, during summer, the popular Vineyard Hopper allows you to hop on and off at the cellar doors of your choosing.

Random fact

Waiheke Island was the first community in New Zealand to vote for a nuclear-free zone. It is popularly believed that this stand helped contribute to the whole country becoming nuclear-free under the prime ministership of David Lange in 1987.

● *By Chris Zeiher*

The island is an electric, heady mix set against a Buddha Bar soundtrack: fast yet slow all at the same time – there's nowhere else on earth quite like it

ROBIN BUSH © GETTY IMAGES

Festivals & events

The Fullers Waiheke Island Wharf2Wharf run, set to take place on 16 January, is one of New Zealand's most unique fun runs, featuring four different distances, the longest 25km, and open to runners and walkers of all abilities with starting points dotted all over the island.

A recent resurgence in popularity has seen the Onetangi Beach Races become a highlight of the Auckland summer social calendar. The event takes places in late February and features races for horses, tractors and amphibious vehicles.

The Waiheke Vintage Festival, held annually in March, celebrates the first picking of the year's vintage with a schedule of about 40 events. Showcasing winemaking, fresh New Zealand produce and music, the events are staged at 19 of the island's wineries.

CLIMB 268 ROCK-HEWN STEPS TO
VISIT THE MEDIEVAL CHAPEL OF
SAINT-MICHEL D'AIGUILHE

BEST IN
TRAVEL
2016

The Auvergne, France

The Auvergne arouses a most delicious kind of vertigo. Its glacier-carved valleys and volcanic peaks are more reminiscent of Iceland than the heart of France

ACTIVITIES | CULTURE | FOOD

Population: **1.4m**

Foreign visitors per year: **350,000**

Main city: **Clermont-Ferrand**

Language: **French**

Major industries: **agriculture, logging, aeronautics, life sciences**

Unit of currency: **euro (€)**

Cost index: **return ticket for the Panoramique des Dômes €11 (US$12), three-course gourmet menu €22 (US$23), double room in a cosy auberge €70 (US$74), a day of learning to paraglide €180 (US$190)**

Why go in 2016?
> *Fresh styles and flavours in France's rustic heart*

The Auvergne arouses a most delicious kind of vertigo. Its glacier-carved valleys and volcanic peaks are more reminiscent of Iceland than the heart of France, but somehow it has long been overlooked for being too peaceably rural. But that's all changing, as French travellers weary of tourist-clogged rivieras seek escape here. The Auvergne has responded by reinventing itself with ambitious art projects and a portfolio of wilderness adventures, without ever losing its small-town charisma.

Conceptual art is being woven into some of the Auvergne's loveliest natural

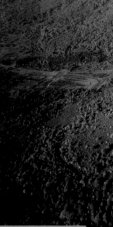

spaces, thanks to the Horizons series: think ghostly sculptures hanging between trees, oversized lilypads and phosphorescent wolves. As a new audience of art lovers streams towards the Auvergne, the region's older gems are being restored and rediscovered. Great news for the Auvergne's eye-popping Romanesque churches and medieval ruins.

Where there's cutting-edge art, creative menus are sure to follow. The Auvergne's reputation for carb-heavy mountain cuisine is being challenged by more inventive fare. And between strolling medieval streets and watching buzzards on a mountain hike, there are plenty of ways to work up an appetite.

Life-changing experiences

■ The Chaîne des Puys, a 40km chain of craters and lava domes, has slumbered for millennia – but its ancient eruptions have bestowed remarkable scenery on the Auvergne. At the Roches Tuilière and Sanadoire, ragged hunks of phonolite stone pierce a carpet of green. And from the region's most popular scenic lookout, the 1465m-high Puy de Dôme, hikers can gaze at cinder cones bubbling towards the misty horizon. Walking trails spiral around the area, but thrillseekers prefer the view from a paraglider.

■ The Clermont-Ferrand region not only has volcanic origins, its gargoyle-draped Notre-Dame cathedral is built entirely out of dark volcanic rock. The city's Basilique

Festivals & events

Be dazzled by dozens of short films at Clermont-Ferrand's International Short Film Festival from 5-13 February.

Throughout the summer specially commissioned artwork will sprout around the Massif Sancy's natural spaces, from ghostly chapels to installations overhanging waterfalls.

Break out of your spectator seat in the third week of August for Aurillac's International Street Theatre Festival.

Be teleported back to the Renaissance at Le Puy-en-Velay's Festival du Roi de l'Oiseau on the third weekend of September.

From the region's most popular lookout, hikers can gaze at cinder cones bubbling towards the misty horizon

Notre-Dame du Port also has smouldering stonework, with volcanic rock layered into intricate floral designs. For more architectural splendour, peer inside Glaine-Montaigut's Romanesque St-Jean church or stroll the ramparts of Montpeyroux.

■ Bring a camera and keen eyes for hikes in the Réserve Naturelle de Chastreix-Sancy. These peaks and plains are home to scores of mountain goats and wild sheep, as well as whistling marmots and birds of prey.

BEST IN TRAVEL 2016

THE CHAÎNE DES PUYS VOLCANIC
MOUNTAIN RANGE REACHES ITS HIGHEST
POINT AT PUY DE DÔME (COMPLETE WITH
ITS CROWNING TELEVISION ANTENNA)

PICAVET © GETTY IMAGES

Most bizarre sight

Ancient spirituality has left its mark on the Auvergne. A Gallo-Roman temple atop the Puy de Dôme, thought to date back to around 140AD, is thought to have been the site of one of the largest places of worship in the western Roman Empire.

Defining difference

The T-shirts and postcards say it best: *'Ici commence l'Auvergne, ici finit la France.'* ('This is where the Auvergne starts and France finishes.') The Auvergne's dour humour is legendary, and friendliness – though gruffly expressed – glints through in every encounter. Say *adieu* to impatient waiters and tense traffic jams; here you'll find leisurely wit and traffic-obstructing cattle.

Regional flavours

Food pilgrims continue to ply the Auvergne's Route des Fromages to tick off the region's five protected designation-of-origin cheeses. Hefty meals like the *truffade*, a mouth-watering meld of duck fat glazed potatoes and cheese, are still hauled onto plates. But chefs are reinventing the Auvergne's cuisine with lighter interpretations of local flavours, like honey-glazed pigeon and pear sorbet. Carnivorous France may seem an unlikely candidate for plant-based cuisine, but a food foraging movement is beginning to enrich palates with vegetarian and vegan alternatives. Nature tour operator Aluna Voyages is steering visitors to source salads from meadows and hunt for blackberries and edible flowers: a thoroughly refreshing reason to say *bon appétit.* ● *By Anita Isalska*

Trending topic

Wolf sightings in the Massif Central have nature lovers excitedly polishing their binoculars. Wolves and bears were once commonplace here, and some of the region's place names even have a pawprint from that era (like Orcival from *vallée de l'ours,* 'bear valley'). For hikers, the few wolves seen scouting the region might herald a return to the Auvergne's primeval past. Understandably, local sheep farmers are less than thrilled.

BEST IN
TRAVEL
2016

CATCH SOME WAVES IN
HAWAII, THE BIRTHPLACE
OF BIG WAVE SURFING

Hawaii, USA

Golden sand beaches, emerald mountain peaks and a relaxed, laid-back attitude – Hawaii is an easy sell

ADVENTURE | FOOD | ACTIVITIES

Population: **1.4 million**
Foreign visitors per year: **3.3 million**
Main town: **Honolulu**
Languages: **English, Hawaiian**
Major industry: **tourism**
Unit of currency: **US dollar (US$)**
Cost index: **1lb bag of 100% Kona coffee US$36, hotel double from US$100, short taxi ride US$10, private surfing lesson US$125**

Why go in 2016? > *There's more to Hawaii than ever before*

Golden sand beaches, emerald mountain peaks and a relaxed, laid-back attitude – Hawaii is an easy sell. Once considered a destination for just sand and surf, these islands are now also attracting visitors for their food, history and adventure. Hawaii Regional Cuisine, a culinary movement that began in the '90s, has matured into a fully fledged way of life, combining the islands' fusion of ethnic flavours with ingredients found on the archipelago. Eat your way through locally sourced menus in Honolulu's hot Chinatown restaurants, sip a farm-to-cup coffee on a Maui agricultural tour or grab a Hawaiian plate lunch at a bustling farmers' market on O'ahu.

Festivals & events

Starting on Easter Sunday, Hilo on the Big Island celebrates Hawaiian art and culture for a week with hula competitions at the Merrie Monarch Festival, honouring King David Kalakaua, who was known for his patronage of the arts.

The Kapalua Wine and Food Festival on Maui takes place over four days in June and features acclaimed chefs and sommeliers.

From 1st to 10th September, scientists, policymakers and NGOs will convene in Honolulu for the IUCN World Conservation Congress, with lots of lectures and workshops on environmental issues.

↑

What's hot...
Craft beer and spirits, food trucks, going green

—

What's not...
Hawaii's cost of living, the Puna lava flow, feral pigs

↓

BEST IN TRAVEL 2016

This year is also a red-letter year for some of the archipelago's biggest attractions. Two national parks, Haleakalā National Park on Maui and Hawai'i Volcanoes National Park on the Big Island, both become centenarians in 2016. And history buffs will already know that 2016 marks the 75th anniversary of the attack on Pearl Harbor. Expect special exhibits and publications to commemorate these events.

Combine all this with Hawaii's ongoing reputation as adventure central – hiking along the smoking crevasse of a volcano, swimming among kaleidoscopic tropical fish or catching a giant roller on O'ahu's North Shore – and you have the right mix to make Hawaii one of 2016's best destinations.

IN HALEAKALĀ NATIONAL PARK, PELE'S PAINT BOX – NAMED FOR THE HAWAIIAN GODDESS OF FIRE AND VOLCANOES – BLAZES WITH SHADES OF RED, YELLOW AND GREY

Life-changing experience

Perhaps nothing will better remind you that the
Hawaiian Islands are very much alive than getting
close to the Big Island's beating heart – Kilauea
Volcano. Feel the heat of one of the world's most
active volcanoes, and witness the Big Island get
bigger at a lake of lava, sulphuric steam vents and
rippled lava tubes.

Trending topic

Sustainability. The islands are precariously
dependent on the outside world – nearly 90% of
Hawaii's food is imported and almost all of its
energy production is dependent on fossil fuels –
but island communities are seeking change. The
local-food movement is strong in Hawaii, and
bumper stickers reading 'buy local; it matters!' are
common. Renewable energy initiatives are popping
up all over the islands. Wind and wave energy on
Maui, geothermal power on the Big Island and
solar panels across the archipelago are all signs
that the islands are on track to achieve their goal
of 70% energy self-sufficiency by 2030. Indeed,
with the financial backing of tech billionaire Larry
Ellison, the small central island of Lana'i hopes to
become a self-sufficient dreamland of electric cars,
sustainable agriculture and green energy.

Random facts

■ Standing tall at 10,200m (33,500ft, measured
from its base on the sea floor), Mauna Kea is
arguably the world's tallest mountain – nearly
a mile taller than Everest.
■ Hawaii has the largest per capita consumption
of Spam (the canned meat) in the USA.
■ The state fish of Hawaii is a mouthful – locally
known as *humuhumunukunukuāpua'a*, but
often referred to as the reef triggerfish.

Most bizarre sight

Fourteen thousand native plants make up the
world's largest garden maze: 4km of winding
paths through the Dole Pineapple Plantation.
The record of completion is just seven minutes,
but it takes the average visitor about an hour to
make their way through.

Defining difference

Nearly 3900km from the nearest land, Hawaii is
one of the world's most isolated archipelagoes –
and one of its most diverse. Before the arrival of
humans, the islands were populated only by species
hardy enough to cross the sea. Left alone, these
early inhabitants evolved into the animals that
exist here today. As a result, over 90% of native
Hawaiian wildlife is found nowhere else on earth.
● *By Alex Howard*

THE MODEL FOR DISNEY'S SLEEPING
BEAUTY CASTLE, NEUSCHWANSTEIN
CASTLE DRIPS WITH FAIRYTALE GLAMOUR

BEST IN
TRAVEL
2016

Bavaria, Germany

An off-the-charts tapestry of tourist treats unfolds between the mighty Alps and the undulating vineyards of Franconia

ACTIVITIES | CULTURE | EVENTS

Population: **12.6 million**

Main town: **Munich**

Language: **German**

Major industries: **automotive, IT, tourism**

Unit of currency: **euro (€)**

Cost index: **1L mug of beer €6-8 (US$6.60-8.80), mid-range hotel double from €70 (US$76), Bavarian Alps ski pass per day €20-44 (US$22-48), sausage in a bun €2 (US$2.20)**

Why go in 2016? › *Bavarias's boisterous beer birthday*

Bavaria is the supermodel among Germany's 16 states, disproportionately blessed with good looks, abundant charisma and an easy-going manner. An off-the-charts tapestry of tourist treats unfolds between the mighty Alps and the undulating vineyards of Franconia. The storybook castles of 'Mad' King Ludwig II poke through dark forest, walled medieval villages line up for inspection along the Romantic Road, and Nazi-era vestiges in Nuremberg and Berchtesgaden let you ponder one of history's most sinister periods. Meanwhile Bavaria's capital, Munich, bewitches with its sweeping gardens, superb museums, grand palaces and

Oktoberfest, the world's biggest beer bash.

Beer is also the focus in 2016 when Bavaria celebrates the 500th anniversary of the Beer Purity Law. The original law, formulated by local dukes in 1516, permitted only barley, hops and water in brewing the amber nectar. The goal was to stop the addition of ox bile, oak bark, henbane and other potentially toxic ingredients more typically found in an alchemist's garden. It is thus considered the world's oldest nutritional law still in effect. So proud of it is

the German Brewers' Union that it has applied to Unesco to designate it a world cultural treasure in time for the significant anniversary.

Life-changing experiences

■ Munich dazzles with its royal palaces, sweeping parks, superb museums and boisterous beer halls. To soak up some local flavour hang out in the hip Glockenbach quarter or watch a home game of world-class soccer team FC Bayern München in the stunning Allianz Arena.

■ On a drive southwest of Munich you'll hit the Bavarian sightseeing jackpot. Clustering at the foot of the big-shouldered Alps are such soul-stirring sights as the richly frescoed Wieskirche pilgrimage church, the woodcarvers' village of Oberammergau, the skiers' paradise of Garmisch-Partenkirchen and, of course, Neuschwanstein Palace, which provided the inspiration for Disney's Sleeping Beauty's castle.

Current craze

Aristocratic holidays. No. You won't be able to have breakfast in Neuschwanstein, but you can ramble around or even spend the night in castles or manor houses still owned or inhabited by Bavarian blue bloods, including Dennenlohe Palace, home of the 'Green Baron'.

Trending topic

A fierce debate rages on whether the Munich Institute for Contemporary History should publish

MICHAEL TAYLOR © GETTY IMAGES

LET YOUR HAIR DOWN WITH SOME BAVARIAN BEERS AT THE LEGENDARY ANNUAL OKTOBERFEST FESTIVAL (LEDERHOSEN OPTIONAL)

'Beer in Bavaria' is the theme of this year's Bavarian State Exhibition that takes over the exuberantly baroque Aldersbach Abbey near Passau from late April to October.

In July, Munich celebrates the 500th anniversary of the Beer Purity Law with an epic three-day party featuring brass bands, culinary treats, a giant beer barrel and beer from 100 Bavarian breweries.

Jostle for tent space at Oktoberfest, Munich's legendary beer-swilling party, between mid-September and early October.

> **Whether in the beer hall or on the ski slope, Bavarians sure know how to let their hair down**

an annotated edition of Adolf Hitler's infamous manifesto, *Mein Kampf,* for educational purposes after the expiration of its state-owned copyright at the end of 2015. Printing or distributing the racist, anti-Semitic tome has been illegal in Germany since the end of WWII.

Most bizarre sight

The Eagle's Nest, a mountain retreat above Berchtesgaden built for Hitler on his 50th birthday, is now a restaurant with show-stopping Alpine vistas.

Defining difference

Quite distinct from the rest of Germany, Bavaria can be as broad-minded as the view from the Zugspitze on a clear day and as narrow as the cobbled lanes threading through medieval Rothenburg ob der Tauber. Its people cherish their dirndl-and-lederhosen traditions while enthusiastically embracing high-tech and innovation. Blue-chip companies like BMW, Adidas, and Siemens fuel its powerful economic engine, yet all this efficiency is diluted by an almost Mediterranean joie de vivre. Whether in the beer hall or on the ski slope, Bavarians sure know how to let their hair down.

Regional flavours

The Chinese say you can eat every part of a pig bar the 'oink' and Bavarian chefs seem to be in full agreement. No part of the animal is spared as they cook up its knuckles, ribs, tongue and belly. Most sausages are pork-based too, with the iconic *Weisswurst* also containing veal. Other typical non-pork staples include *Hendl* (roast chicken), *Brezn* (pretzels) and *Obatzda* (soft cheese), all of which populate the menus of atmospheric beer halls or gardens. A meal special to Bavaria is the *Brotzeit* (literally 'bread time'), a cold snack of bread, sausage and cheese usually eaten in the afternoon or early evening.

● *By Andrea Schulte-Peevers*

ESCAPE THE CROWDS AND HEAD FOR THE VERDANT COASTLINE NEAR VILA DO ABRAÃO AT ILHA GRANDE

Costa Verde, Brazil

Costa Verde is a stretch of unspoiled shoreline featuring emerald peaks, peaceful islands, crashing waterfalls and stunning, near-deserted beaches

ADVENTURE | OFF-ROAD | ACTIVITIES

Population: **270,000**
Main town: **Angra dos Reis**
Languages: **Portuguese**
Major industry: **tourism**
Unit of currency: **Brazilian real (R$)**
Cost index: caipirinha **R$7 (US$2), hotel double R$140 (US$43), scuba diving per day R$195 (US$60), pair of Havaianas flip flops R$28 (US$8), return bus ticket from Rio de Janeiro City to Paraty R$70 (US$21)**

Why go in 2016? > *Remote antidote to Rio Olympic fever*

In 2016, the Summer Olympic Games in Rio de Janeiro City may be Brazil's biggest draw, but you'll find a lesser-known paradise just westward of the famous oceanside metropolis. Costa Verde ('green coast') is a stretch of unspoiled shoreline featuring emerald peaks, peaceful islands, crashing waterfalls and stunning, near-deserted beaches. Rio and São Paulo may get most of the limelight in Brazil, but a trip to Costa Verde is fully warranted in its own right.

The Rio–Santos stretch of the BR-101 highway runs through a corridor of verdant *Mata Atlântica* (Portuguese for Atlantic rainforest) and it may be the last paved road you see once you settle in on Costa Verde's shores. You'll wear the soles of your Havaianas thin taking everything in by foot – no cars save for taxis are allowed on the cobbled streets of the Unesco-listed colonial town of Paraty. The same goes for Vila do Abraão, the main beachfront hamlet of the region's biggest island, Ilha Grande; the only vehicles you'll see are the town's single police car, garbage truck and fire engine.

Costa Verde is a paradise of untouched natural wonders. Ilha Grande Bay is peppered with approximately 365 government-protected islands, most of which are uninhabited. The island retreat of Ilha Grande owes its pristine condition to its history as a pirate's lair, a leper colony and finally a penitentiary for political prisoners and some of Brazil's most treacherous criminals. This shady past deterred developers for a long time, which is just as well – you'd best get here now before everyone catches on.

Life-changing experiences

■ Dreaming of a deserted ocean utopia? Costa Verde is ideal for leisurely nature lovers and adrenaline junkies alike. Dawdle the days away exploring wild, natural beaches, or take your pick of adventure activities: hike the rugged jungle hills, kayak secluded tropical fjords, or strap on snorkel or scuba gear and swim with tropical fish. Costa Verde's translucent jade waters are a spectacular natural aquarium.

Festivals & events

Ring in 2016 in maritime style in Angra dos Reis, a region with some of Costa Verde's most luxurious hotels and private islands. Ships and boats from near and far dock here for the Procissão Maritima, a carnival-at-sea on 1 January. A prize is given for the most creatively decorated boat.

As carnival festivities rage on in Rio de Janeiro City, earthier types get down and dirty in Paraty for the wild but simple Bloco da Lama (Mud Carnival, 6 February). There's very little pomp at this party – participants commune with nature by smearing black mud from the lagoon all over their bodies to honour an ancient local practice traditionally performed to cure the ill.

In Paraty, four days in August are dedicated to the country's famous cachaça in the Festival da Cachaça, Cultura e Sabores. Representatives from local *alambiques* (distilleries) set up tasting kiosks in the town centre. There are also shows of samba and *ciranda* (a traditional song and dance genre, characterised by large circles of dancers).

> **You'll wear the soles of your Havaianas thin taking everything in by foot – no cars save for taxis are allowed on the cobbled streets of Paraty**

PARATY'S COBBLESTONED STREETS, GALLERIES AND SHOPS ARE PERFECT STROLLING TERRITORY

■ Paraty is the end of one of the routes of the Estrada Real (Royal Road), a colonial-era network of paths leading from the Minas Gerais and São Paulo states to the port towns of Rio de Janeiro state. Gold, diamonds and other precious minerals that were discovered in the country's interior were transported along the Estrada Real to the coast for export back to Portugal during the 16th, 17th and 18th centuries. Today, visitors to Brazil can take a pilgrimage along the same routes by foot or on horseback.

■ Take a jeep ride down Paraty's Gold Road – a route once used to export gold from Minas Gerais – and stop to sip some cachaça, a sugarcane rum and the main ingredient in the caipirinha, Brazil's national cocktail. Paraty is known for producing some of the finest cachaça in the country. Maria Izabel, about 10km north of town, is among the best distilleries and often places highly in national tasting contests.

Regional flavours

You'll savour some of Brazil's best seafood in Costa Verde. *Moqueca*, a Brazilian fish stew, is a staple all along the coast of the country. In this part of Brazil, *moqueca* can also feature shrimp or calmari. It's served with a sprinkling of *farofa* (toasted cassava flour) and best washed down with a *caipirinha* or a juice made from exotic fruits such as *pitanga*, *cajá* or *cupuaçu*. ● *By MaSovaida Morgan*

BEST IN
TRAVEL
2016

ST HELENA'S ROCK
FORMATIONS ARE AS
FASCINATING TO ROCK BUFFS
TODAY AS THEY WERE TO
DARWIN TWO CENTURIES AGO

St Helena, British Territories

This über-isolated island will suddenly be part of the planet less lonely when its much-talked-about airport finally opens in 2016

OFF-ROAD | ADVENTURE | FOOD

Population: **4,442**

Foreign visitors per year: **2,800 (projected to increase to around 10,700 within four years of the airport opening)**

Languages: **English, with a distinctive Saints' patois**

Unit of currency: **St Helena pound (£), pegged at 1:1 with the pound sterling**

Cost index: **cup of coffee £1 (US$1.50), guesthouse room from £55 per night with breakfast (US$82), Ford Escort rental car £10-12 (US$15-18) per day, wi-fi £6 (US$9) per hour**

10

Why go in 2016? › *Experience a moment of evolution on an ultra-remote Atlantic island*

'A little world, within itself, which excites our curiosity.' That was how Charles Darwin saw St Helena when he visited in 1836, but this über-isolated island – the faintest of paradisiacal punctuation points on the bright blue page of the South Atlantic Ocean – will suddenly be part of the planet less lonely when its much-talked-about airport finally opens in 2016. Previously the only way to visit (save on your own boat) was by sailing 3100km from Cape Town on the RMS *Saint Helena* – a 10-day return trip – but soon it'll be possible to arrive in 5.5 hours from Johannesburg, and a new

32-bedroom hotel is being built on Jamestown Main St to accommodate extra travellers. For some, St Helena's inaccessibility is a major part of its appeal, but remoteness is both blessing and curse. Islanders have watched the economic viability of their cut-off community slowly evaporate ever since the age of mass air travel took off, and most view the development with a mixture of excitement and trepidation. The airport will doubtless change St Helena eventually, but it won't make it any less exciting or curious as a destination in the short term. Mobile phone reception will remain a rumour, cars will be decades behind the times, drivers will still wave when passing and island life, including the unique flora and fauna that so intrigued Darwin, will continue at its own somnambulant pace. Sure, visitor numbers will rise, but as Charlie would point out, that's evolution for you.

What's hot...
Future proofing

———

What's not...
Brain-draining emigration

Festivals & events

Commemorate the 195th anniversary of Napoleon's death on the island during the slightly surreal Moment de Memoir, which takes place beside the French Emperor's empty tomb on 5 May.

Celebrate the 514th anniversary of the island's discovery with a St Helena Day shindig on 21 May.

© ST HELENA TOURISM

Life-changing experiences

Drive around in a rental car straight out of the *Sweeney*, waving to everyone you pass, and then park up and explore by foot. The island's 'Postbox Walks' wend around rugged cliff tops, through cloud forests and hidden valleys to volcanic peaks – but be warned, the terrain can be tough and the ascents vertiginous. There's plenty to look out for, though. Known as the Galápagos of the South Atlantic, St Helena has spent 14 million years in glorious geographic isolation and boasts about 500 endemic species not found anywhere else in the world, including the eccentric St Helena plover. In the sea, you can dive, snorkel or simply swim with an astonishing array of exotic marine life – from playful dolphins to whale sharks, which regularly cruise past in January, and humpback whales (commonly seen June to October).

SLOW AND STEADY WINS THE RACE: JONATHAN, A SEYCHELLES GIANT TORTOISE, HAS RACKED UP A STAGGERING 183 YEARS OF AGE

Trending topic
How the island will handle a predicted four-fold increase in visitor numbers.

Most bizarre sight
Meet Jonathan, St Helena's celebrity giant tortoise – who began tottering around the island just a few years after Napoleon died.

Defining difference
The island is part of British Overseas Territory St Helena, Ascension and Tristan da Cunha – a super-loose collection of isles and atolls scattered across 3642km of otherwise empty Atlantic Ocean.

Local lingo
Although the island is English speaking, the local Saints' accent, sentence structure and dialect is distinct – sounding something like a cross between Yoda and an 18th-century English pirate. Islanders might say 'Who you is?', instead of 'Who are you?', and 'Eierce, I'm gorn home for my bita dinner' translates as 'Yes, I'm going home for dinner'.

Regional flavours
'The only good thing about St Helena is the coffee', Napoleon allegedly sulkily said after being placed in exile here following his defeat at Waterloo. We think there's plenty more to like – not least the sensational tuna fishcakes that are the island's signature dish, best washed down with a splash of Tungi, a cactus pear-based locally distilled liquor – but the Little Corporal clearly knew a good cuppa when he sipped one. St Helena coffee beans (from plants originally sown on the island by the East India Company in 1733) are among the best – and most expensive – in the world. Grab a brew at the island's Coffee Shop, or a buy a bottle of Midnight Mist coffee liqueur.

● *By Patrick Kinsella*

Lonely Planet's
Top 10
Cities

© SHUTTERSTOCK

BEYOND KOTOR'S OLD
CITY WALLS, VERDANT
LIMESTONE MOUNTAINS
LOOM

Kotor, Montenegro

In Kotor's maze of alleyways and church-fronted plazas there's just one thing to do: get lost and experience local life

CULTURE | FOOD | ACTIVITIES

Population: **23,000**
Foreign visitors per year: **372,360**
Language: **Montenegrin**
Unit of currency: **euro (€)**
Cost index: **takeaway bottle of wine €10 (US$10.85), apartment for a night €50-150 (US$54-163), vintage Balkan magic carpet €75-1500 (US$80-1060)**

1

Why go in 2016? > *Before it gets the cruise ship makeover*

Hemmed in on all sides by dramatic folds of rock, it's nigh-on impossible to take a photo in Kotor where looming mountains aren't loitering in a corner of the frame. It's got to be said that it's a picture-perfect visage from virtually every angle. Beyond its historical city walls is the much-loved Bay of Kotor, gorgeous and about as fjordlike as the Mediterranean can get without qualifying as a legitimate fjord.

But what lies within is just as memorable: a living, breathing town where locals catch up over strong coffee at pavement cafes on cobbled squares, queue for warm bread at the bakers and get their shoes repaired at the traditional cobblers. Here in Kotor's maze of alleyways and church-fronted plazas there's just one thing to do: get lost and experience local life. Forget restaurants – the flavours of Kotor are brought to life in its shops and local produce market, cloistered within the walls of the Stari Grad (Old Town). Here you can sample cheeses smoked with walnuts or pistachios, dollops of golden honey and meaty hams, then seek out enthusiastic locals in tiny wine shops to recommend stonking good reds bottled on their doorstep.

Kotor is often called a 'mini Dubrovnik', but that hardly does it justice. In fact, as its big brother in Croatia becomes more and more beholden to hordes of cruise ship tourists, that moniker feels more like a disservice. In reality the comparison is most likely a crystal ball for it seems as though more and more southern Europe cruises want to stop at Kotor's diminutive port. But with such a stunning sapphire bay, it's no surprise that everyone wants a piece of the action.

Thankfully, the hordes of now-you-see-them, now-you-don't tourists that flit on and off the boats have yet to leave a permanent mark on this quaint town. Cruise souvenir shops are in short supply and within the fortified walls, Kotor's Stari Grad still has the air of a comfy home. How long this charmed life will continue is anyone's guess, but if Dubrovnik is anything to go by, the clock is ticking.

> *Here you can sample cheeses smoked with walnuts or pistachios, dollops of golden honey and meaty hams, then seek out enthusiastic locals in tiny wine shops to recommend stonking good reds*

Festivals & events

Masquerade balls... concerts... generally raucous revelry in February – is this Venice? No, it's Kotor's annual Winter Carnival and the biggest date in the calendar this side of Christmas.

Boka Night, a 300-year-old beauty pageant in mid-August, is about fabulously bedecked boats competing on the boka (bay). Song and dance reverberate through the alleys of the Stari Grad and the night culminates in a winner being picked, crowned by festive fireworks on the harbourfront.

WITH ITS LABYRINTHINE LANES AND PIAZZAS, KOTOR TOWN IS A TREASURE WEDGED IN A MOUNTAIN VALLEY

Life-changing experiences

- It's a 1200m hike up the town fortifications' crumbling steps to get to the lookout point on St John's Hill. Only sections of the original wall remain climbable; make it up to the teeny church dangling cliffside and you'll be greeted with sweeping views of the bay.

- Exploring the bay and its romantic villages by boat, it's easy to see why Romans built their villas here and Venetians graced its shores with palazzos. Floating in the centre is Our-Lady-of-the-Rocks – a 15th-century island, home to a frescoed church and an ice-cream pitstop.

- Twenty-five hairpin bends curling up the back road to Mt Lovćen have got to be one of the best drives on the planet. Prepare to pull over many times, because from up here the bayside panorama just gets better with every turn.

Most bizarre sight

Clinging to the rock face like a brooding bony dragon's tail, no guidebook can prepare you for that first neck-craning glimpse of Kotor's fortifications, which began creeping almost vertically up the Lovćen massif behind town in the 9th century. Take that, Escher.

Best shopping

Venetian, Austrian and Yugoslav rule have all contributed to a truckload of treasure that still resides in Kotor's dens of antiquities. Fine Balkan rugs, delicate Mediterranean laces, Art Nouveau pots and historical garb all vie for space in the town's kooky antiques shops, tucked behind unmarked doors in hidden lanes and squares.

● *By Lorna Parkes*

What's hot...
Resurrected plans to construct a cable car from Kotor to the former royal capital of Cetinje via towering Lovćen. If the government pulls it off, the views will be tremendous.

What's not...
Derelict buildings. Such a blot on the landscape – particularly that fine concrete specimen across from the gateway to Kotor's Stari Grad. Will the government ever knock them down?

QUITO'S METROPOLITAN
CATHEDRAL IS THE OFFICIAL
CATHEDRAL OF ECUADOR

Quito, Ecuador

Quito's Old Town is an architectural treasure trove – yet the soaring mountain setting makes it breathtaking

ADVENTURE | CULTURE | VALUE

Population: **2.7 million**
Foreign visitors per year: **680,000**
Languages: **Spanish, Kichwa**
Unit of currency: **US dollar (US$)**
Altitude: **2850m**
Cost index: **hotel double/dorm room US$75/12, airport to Old Town taxi ride US$26, return cable car ride US$8.50, cup of coffee US$1, artisan chocolate bar US$4**

Why go in 2016? > Wheels of fortune...

Oil money surges in with more force than the Amazon's headwaters. While the cash keeps getting injected into sprucing up this Unesco-listed smorgasbord of South American colonial architecture, the glory days are likely to be ahead of Quito as well as behind it. Time might seem to stand still in Quito's historical centre, which harks back to the 16th century, and in the tradition-steeped mountains around, but the snazzy modern face of the city could be what entices you in 2016.

All that colonial charm will become a whole lot more navigable, with Quito's much-hyped metro system poised to roll – whisking wannabe visitors from

QUITO'S OLD TOWN IS PEPPERED WITH ARCHITECTURAL GEMS LIKE THE GOTHIC BASÍLICA DEL VOTO NACIONAL.

JOHN AND TINA REID © GETTY IMAGES

the bus station right through all the historical districts of the city. A refurbished train station and a gleaming new airport have also helped to usher in a swathe of high-end tourists to complement the adventure-seeking backpackers. Scan the events calendar and you'll see major golf and tennis tournaments running as well as those volcano treks; cast your eye at the skyline to see dynamic constructions like the new Union of South American Nations building contrast with centuries-old churches.

Confidence is on a high and the quality of city accommodation is on the up too. 2016 will see the new airport garner its first on-site hotel (the Wyndham Gran Condor), and of the others set to follow in its wake, the most exciting is the project to rejuvenate one of Quito's original hotels, the historical centre's Casa Perez Pallares. Tourists might flock to the Mitad del Mundo, the equatorial line lying just north of the city, to stand with a foot in each hemisphere, but the main divide in Quito is between the very ancient and the very modern.

Life-changing experiences

Quito's Old Town is an architectural treasure trove – yet the soaring mountain setting makes it breathtaking (and breath-sapping):
■ Explore the seat of the Ecuadorian Presidency (current incumbent Rafael Correa) at ornate Palacio del Gobierno, known for its striking mural of Orellana descending the Amazon.

Festivals & events

August 10th marks the day Ecuadorians first rose up against the Spanish seeking independence, and it was in Quito that the revolution began. Independence Day celebrations roll on all month: exhibitions, concerts, general merriment...

Andean pipe music? Look elsewhere for tradition: December's Quitofest embraces the bold, the brave and the bizarre of the independent music scene, with the latest Ecuadorian talent augmented by international celebs.

It's getting on for 500 years since the Spanish first hit Ecuador: as if the Founding of the City Festival needed an excuse to get even more riotous. This is the year's big event, held around the foundation day of 6 December: a week-long debauch of feasting, dancing and parading.

■ Gawk at the entrancing chapel-come-museum of Capilla del Hombre, in the Bellavista district.
■ Take the TeléferiQo (cable car) up Volcán Pichincha to 4100m for unforgettable city views.
■ Book your berth on the weekend train up to the base of one of the world's highest active volcanoes, Volcán Cotopaxi.

Trending topics

Street art: not only is it colourful; it's also educational. Quito's urban spaces have recently become a canvas for a new form of language (a hybrid of Spanish and the indigenous tongue, Kichwa) and, better, a couple of grammar vigilantes who pride themselves on correcting other graffiti artists' spelling mistakes have become an attraction in themselves!

Most bizarre sight

Charismatic old monasteries hardly stand out in Quito, but the Convento de San Diego will leave you marvelling at its artwork. As if the unexpected presence of a Hieronymus Bosch painting (everyone's stumped as to how it got here) wasn't odd enough, there is a depiction of the Last Supper with disciples feasting on the Andean speciality of *cuy* (roast guinea pig). Not such a common dish in the Middle East...

Classic restaurant experience

Zazu is at the zenith of modern Ecuadorian cuisine: hang with all the bright young things and chow down on divine ceviche (the citrus-marinated seafood Ecuador and neighbouring Peru are famed for).

Classic place to stay

Period boutique is all the rage now in Quito, but Casa Gangotena spearheaded the trend. This glam 31-room mansion dates from the 1920s but opened as a hotel in 2011 with an intelligent refurbishment that dazzlingly restored its Art Nouveau glory.

● *By Luke Waterson*

BEST IN
TRAVEL
2016

DUBLIN'S RICH MUSICAL
HERITAGE LIVES ON IN ITS
MUSIC BARS

Dublin, Ireland

No longer a dirty auld town, Dublin has a healthy hue – with people embracing its inner green spaces and exploring the wild outdoor arenas along the coast and 'beyond the pale'

CULTURE   ACTIVITIES   EVENTS

Population: **1.3 million**

Foreign visitors per year: **4 million**

Languages: **English – spoken with an unmistakable brogue, Irish**

Unit of currency: **euro (€)**

Cost index: **pint of Guinness €4-6 (US$4.25-6.35), short taxi ride €11 (US$11.66), average museum/historic building entry €7-10 (US$7.40-10.60), B&B double room €60-100 (US$63.50106)**

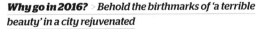

Why go in 2016? *> Behold the birthmarks of 'a terrible beauty' in a city rejuvenated*

Yesterday the economic outlook was as dark as a pint of stout and the shadow of mass emigration again loomed, but today Ireland has bounced back – and nowhere is this buoyancy more evident than on the Liffey's bustling banks. The diaspora has turned inside out and Dublin is now a truly cosmopolitan capital, with an influx of people, energy and ideas infusing the ever-beguiling, multi-layered city with fresh flavours and kaleidoscopic colours. Over 40% of the population is estimated to be under 30 and the place pulsates with youthful vibrancy, optimism and creativity.

No longer a dirty auld town, Dublin has a healthy hue – with people embracing its inner green spaces and exploring the wild outdoor arenas along the coast and 'beyond the pale'.

This year marks the centenary of the 1916 Easter Rising, the moment when – as Nobel Prize-pocketing word sculptor WB Yeats put it – *'All changed, changed utterly: / A terrible beauty is born'*. WB's terrible beauty was the wave of passion, politics and action that washed across Ireland after an armed rebellion against British rule erupted on the streets of Dublin, leaving scars still visible on the city's best-loved buildings. The uprising failed, but ham-fisted executions of its leaders – one carried to the firing squad on a stretcher and another killed hours after marrying his lover in a candlelit ceremony in Kilmainham Gaol – saw public support for the nationalist cause surge, sparking a chain of events that ultimately led to the creation of the Irish Republic. A huge €22-million has been set aside for planning the 2016 celebrations.

Life-changing experiences

Meet the perfect stranger through the Little Museum's brilliant City of a Thousand Welcomes initiative, where an ordinary Dubliner will tell you about their home town over a free drink in a local pub. Follow the Independence Trail around key sites where nation-forming events took place, such as the GPO, Kilmainham Gaol and Dublin Castle. Plunge into

Festivals & events

The 1916 centenary will be commemorated all year, but Easter is the focus for festivities. Exploring five themes – remembrance, reconciliation, imagination, presentation and celebration – planned events range from art exhibitions in the Little Museum to a memorial service at Arbour Hill, culminating with a city-centre parade on Easter Sunday (27 March).

St Patrick's Day (17 March) is a public holiday in Ireland and a de facto national day for people who consider themselves Irish the world over. Amid centenary celebrations, Dublin's 2016 St Patrick's Festival (16-20 March) promises to be massive.

Reflecting Ireland's healthier face, the world's biggest and toughest triathlon – Ironman – arrives in Dublin in 2016.

In honour of James Joyce's epic tome *Ulysses* set entirely on one Dublin day in 1904, the city celebrates Bloomsday on 16 June. For a bloodier bookish shindig, sink your fangs into October's *Dracula*-inspired Bram Stoker Festival.

DAVID SOANES PHOTOGRAPHY © GETTY IMAGES

THE O'CONNELL BRIDGE CROSSES DUBLIN'S RIVER LIFFEY AT THE VERY HEART OF THE CITY

the Irish Sea at the Forty Foot in Sandycove, or nurse a deep dark pint fireside in Mulligan's on Poolbeg St, where the atmosphere is as potent as the stout. Wander amid the leaves of Phoenix Park and St Stephen's Green, along the new 'Dubline' discovery trail, across the hallowed grounds of Trinity College, over Ha'penny Bridge and through Temple Bar to Christchurch, or right out of the city and into the Dublin Mountains – but do wander. Dublin deserves to be imbibed at walking pace.

Current craze

Puckering up to the perfect pint of porter is on everyone's Dublin to-do list, but guess what...not all Irish beer is black. Join the boutique beer revolution at increasingly popular craft ale pubs like The Black Sheep and Against the Grain.

↑

What's hot...
Craft cuisine, local liquor and outdoor fitness

What's not...
Stag parties and paying vastly over-inflated prices in Temple Bar pubs after 11pm

↓

Most bizarre sight

From the Tart with the Cart (Molly Malone statue, temporarily on Suffolk St) and the Stiletto in the Ghetto (Spire of Light, O'Connell St) through to the Prick with the Stick (James Joyce effigy, North Earl St) – in Dublin, public art collides with irreverent street humour like nowhere else.

Classic place to stay

Temple Bar might be boisterous, but at its heart are several classy accommodation options, including the Merchant House and No 25 Eustace Street – a Georgian House which sleeps seven and comes complete with Bechstein boudoir piano and free-standing rolltop bath.

● *By Patrick Kinsella*

BEST IN
TRAVEL
2016

ONE OF PENANG'S LAST
BASTIONS OF THE OLD CHINESE
SETTLEMENTS, THE CLAN
JETTIES FLOATING VILLAGE
BEGAN LIFE IN THE EARLY
19TH CENTURY

George Town, Malaysia

George Town's increasingly modern and arty spin is a fascinating counterpoint to its historical Unesco World Heritage-listed streetscape

FOOD   CULTURE   EVENTS

Population: **800,000**
Foreign visitors per year: **2.1 million**
Languages: **Malay (Bahasa Malaysia), English**
Unit of currency: **Malaysian ringgit (RM)**
Cost index: **plate of *char kway teow* noodles RM8 (US$2.15), double room in a mid-range boutique hotel RM250 (US$67), bicycle rental per day RM20 (US$5.40), George Town street art smartphone cover RM5 (US$1.35)**

Why go in 2016?
> *A surprising arts scene & hip accommodation*

In the Malaysian state of Penang, George Town's increasingly modern and arty spin is a fascinating counterpoint to its historical Unesco World Heritage-listed streetscape. Initiatives such as the Urban Xchange: Crossing Over festival have inspired the creation of even more funky street art, and an abandoned former transport hub has been repurposed as the Hin Bus Depot Art Centre. Art, film, music and dance all feature at George Town's most versatile exhibition space, and new accommodation such as the Sinkeh boutique guesthouse also provide a haven for the expanding arts scene. With

↑

What's hot...
Monthly *Say It Like You Mean It* sessions from January to August – featuring everything from comedy and poetry to live music – at the Canteen at ChinaHouse.
Every Saturday night, Lebuh Armenian hosts the spontaneity of the ad hoc, al fresco *Armenian Street's Got Talent*.

...What's not
As George Town's heritage architecture becomes increasingly popular for development into cafes, shops and hotels, pressure on the property rights of long-term residents threatens to diminish the bustling, traditional ambience of the area.

↓

a name meaning 'newcomer' in the Hokkien Chinese dialect common in Penang, Sinkeh combines downstairs art studios and performance spaces with coolly minimalist upstairs accommodation. Time your visit with one of the city's regular arts and music festivals to experience one of Asia's most inventive and diverse arts communities.

Life-changing experiences
■ Negotiate the meandering roads and laneways of George Town's historical townscape to discover a compelling outdoor gallery of street art. The surprising scene kicked off in 2010 when the Penang state government sponsored the installation of quirky steel artworks crafted by the Sculptureatwork studio. The quirky cartoon-like sculptures depicting local traditions and culture inject both humour and historical information into George Town's heritage core. In 2012, the George Town Festival commissioned Lithuanian artist Ernest Zacharevic to create bold and playful street art – often incorporating existing objects like bicycles and a motorbike – and Penang's excellent street art scene has been further expanded in following years by both local and international artists.

■ Explore George Town's superb hawker food scene: culinary influences from China, Malaysia, India, Thailand and the region's Peranakan (Straits-Chinese) culture all combine in popular eating hubs around the city. Must-try dishes include tamarind-laced *asam laksa* (a tangy, fish-based noodle soup), and the smokey, stir-fried goodness of *char kway teow* noodles. Consider a street food excursion with Food Tour Penang to taste the best of George Town, and definitely skip lunch to make the most of their evening tours. For recipes to reinvent back home, join a market tour and cooking class at Nazlina Spice Station and learn a few tasty secrets of local Penang cuisine.

GEORGE TOWN'S STREET ART SCENE BEGAN LIFE AS A COMMISSION TO CELEBRATE THE AREA'S RICH HISTORY

Classic restaurant experience

Begin a leisurely evening at Kebaya at Seven Terraces with cocktails amid the heritage vibe of the hotel's Baba Bar, before moving through to the elegant, antique-studded dining room for innovative four-course degustation menus featuring modern updates of classic Indo and Peranakan cuisine.

Classic place to stay

Clove Hall offers accommodation in a restored Anglo-Malay mansion whose site was originally a clove plantation. Six very comfortable suites also incorporate the property's former stables, and luxuriant tropical gardens are dotted with spice trees and stately palms.

● *By Brett Atkinson*

The quirky cartoon-like sculptures depicting local traditions and culture inject both humour and historical information into George Town's heritage core

Festivals & events

Eclectic and interesting short films from the Asia-Pacific region are presented at Tropfest SEA in early February. Screenings take place outdoors on George Town's waterfront Esplanade, and live music and local food complete the laid-back festival atmosphere.

In April, George Town's Esplanade is further enlivened with diverse cultures, beats and melodies at the annual Penang World Music Festival. Countries and genres represented in recent years include South African reggae, Brazilian tribal rhythms and Spanish flamenco guitar.

Every August, the George Town Festival celebrates the city's Unesco World Heritage status with a month-long showcase of music, art, culture and history. Performances and events take place across George Town, many in the city's cafes, restored heritage buildings and colonial streetscapes.

BEST IN
TRAVEL
2016

ROTTERDAM'S SKYLINE
BOASTS A LINE-
UP OF FUTURISTIC
ARCHITECTURE

Rotterdam, the Netherlands

The Netherlands' second-biggest metropolis is a veritable open-air gallery of modern, post-modern and contemporary construction

ACTIVITIES | CULTURE | EVENTS

Population: **1.2 million**

Foreign visitors per year: **425,000**

Language: **Dutch, English widespread**

Unit of currency: **euro (€)**

Cost index: **cup of coffee €2.50 (US$2.72), glass of beer €2.80 (US$3.05), short taxi ride €8 (US$8.70), harbour cruise €11.25 (US$12.23)**

Why go in 2016? > *Riding a wave of urban development, redevelopment and regeneration*

Futuristic architecture, inspired initiatives such as inner-city canal surfing, a proliferation of art, and a surge of drinking, dining and nightlife venues make Rotterdam one of Europe's most exhilarating cities right now.

The Netherlands' second-biggest metropolis, on the vast Nieuwe Maas river, is a veritable open-air gallery of modern, post-modern and contemporary construction. It's a remarkable feat for a city largely razed to the ground by WWII bombers. Rebuilding has continued unabated ever since with ingenuity and vision.

THE WHIMSICAL MARKTHAL BUILDING HOUSES A BUSTLING FOOD HALL

Festivals & events

Stay in unique locations such as art installations and take artist-guided expeditions during mid-April's Motel Mozaïque music, art and performance festival.

Around a thousand musicians perform at mid-July's renowned North Sea Jazz festival.

Rotterdam's multicultural makeup is a vital part of its lifeblood, with some 170 nationalities calling it home. A cacophonous 'battle of drums' and colourful street parade are highlights of the Rotterdam Unlimited Zomercarnaval (Summer Carnival), a vibrant Caribbean celebration in late July.

Tours of normally off-limits industrial areas, as well as nautical displays and sea shanties, are part of early September's fascinating Wereldhavendagen (World Port Days). Festival-goers don retro get-ups such as sailor outfits for the spin-off de Nacht van de Kaap (Night of the Cape), held on one crazy Wereldhavendagen night in Katendrecht, Rotterdam's former red-light quarter.

Eye-popping recent openings include the Markthal Rotterdam, the country's inaugural indoor food market. Its extraordinary inverted-U-shaped design incorporates glass-walled apartments arcing over the foodhall's fantastical 40m-high fruit- and vegetable-muraled ceiling and scores of artisan stalls and eateries.

Other striking skyline additions include the glitzy 'vertical city', De Rotterdam, the Netherlands' largest building, designed by Pritzker-winning Rotterdam architect Rem Koolhaas. Dramatic views from its hotel, cocktail-bar terrace and restaurant take in the Erasmusbrug – the swooping white cable-stayed bridge dubbed 'De Zwaan' (The Swan).

Among Rotterdam's innovative redevelopments is Station Hofplein – the former station of the disused Hofpleinlijn railway, whose viaduct arches are transforming into cultural and creative spaces. Openings here have so far included cutting-edge restaurants, boutiques and a jazz club. Station

Hofplein is connected to the city centre by the wooden Luchtsingel ('air canal') footbridge over the train tracks, which was propelled by crowd-funding (selling inscribed planks). One section of the bridge skewers the office-building-turned-design-studio-hub Schieblock, topped by the pioneering DakAkker harvestable roof, producing fruit, vegetables and honey.

Early 2016 sees the Museum Rotterdam open inside the 'cloud-like' Rem Koolhaas-designed Timmerhuis, showcasing Rotterdam's past, present and future.

And from late 2016, Europe's busiest port – already on the Paris–Amsterdam high-speed rail line – will become more accessible than ever when direct Eurostar services linking London with Amsterdam stop at the stunning new skylit, stainless steel-encased Rotterdam Centraal train station.

Life-changing experiences

■ Explore Rotterdam's seafaring heritage at maritime museums or on a harbour cruise past its shipyards' colossal cranes and containers.
■ Delve into historical neighbourhoods that escaped wartime destruction, such as charming gabled-and-windmilled Delfshaven (the America-bound Pilgrims prayed at the church next door to Delfshaven's wonderful canal-side brewery, Stadsbrouwerij De Pelgrim).
■ Encounter exceptional art at the masterpiece-filled Museum Boijmans van Beuningen; the Kunsthal Rotterdam's diverse exhibitions; and attention-grabbing sculptures throughout the city's streets and squares.
■ Hit pumpin' clubs such as the 6000-capacity Maassilo, inside a century-old grain silo.

Current craze

Surf's up! From 2016, surfers, bodyboarders, stand-up paddleboarders and kayakers can take a wild 14-second ride on a naturally purified, barrelling 1.5m-high wave in the city-centre Steigersgracht canal (its water-level beach-house cafe provides up-close views of the action). Locals voted for it in a municipal 'city initiative' competition; profits are directed into similar projects.

Trending topic

Staying dry. Efforts to make the city – 80% of which lies below sea level – fully climate-proof by 2035 include water plazas that double as playgrounds, car park water storage tanks and environmentally sustainable floating houses.

Most bizarre sight

Mind-bending late 20th-century icons include the Overblaak development's surreal 'forest' of 45-degree-tilted, hexagonal-pylon-mounted cube-shaped apartments (one's now a museum, another a Stayokay backpacker hostel).

Best shopping

Brand-name shops line the bustling, outdoor, semi-subterranean Beurstraverse (nicknamed De Koopgoot, 'buying trench'); alternative options congregate on and around Meent. For made-in-Rotterdam fashion, homewares, books and more, browse concept shop Groos (revived local slang for 'pride').

Classic place to stay

A photo finish between Art Nouveau showpiece Hotel New York (the Holland-America passenger ship line's former HQ, with timber-panelled suites in its old boardrooms) and artist-designed King Kong Hostel (a vintage- and industrial-furniture-filled haven on Witte de Withstraat, the city's coolest street). Both, in their own way, reflect Rotterdam's irrepressible spirit. ● *By Catherine Le Nevez*

BEST IN
TRAVEL
2016

GANESH CHATURTHI SEES
MUMBAI'S STREETS FILLED
WITH MUSIC, DRUMMING AND
FIRE CRACKERS UNTIL DEEP
INTO THE NIGHT

Mumbai, India

While downtown floats in a perpetual colonial summer, new towers are shooting up in the burbs faster than you can say Chowpatty Beach

CULTURE · FOOD · EVENTS

Population: **21 million**
Foreign visitors per year: **4 million**
Languages: **English, Marathi, Hindi**
Unit of currency: **Rupee (₹)**
Cost index: **portion of *bhelpuri* (Mumbai-style salad) ₹40 (US$0.64), bottle of Maharashtra wine ₹1500 (US$24), double room in a mid-range hotel ₹1000-4000 (US$16-US$64)**

Why go in 2016? › India, upgraded

Mumbai has long prided itself on being India's 'Maximum City' (credit to author Suketa Mehta for the snappy nickname), and 2016 is set to be the year that this powerhouse of fashion, finance and film comes of age. With India predicted to overtake China as the world's fastest growing economy in 2016, Metro Mumbai is investing its wealth in an unprecedented phase of development and expansion.

The signs can be seen all over the city. Abandoned colonial cotton mills are finding new life as glitzy shopping arcades, where Mumbai's most glamorous residents air-kiss between smart-phone calls, while modelling the latest designs from Rohit Bal and Manish Malhotra. Commuters speed above the streets in air-conditioned comfort on the new Mumbai Monorail. Even Bollywood has set its sights on global domination, meaning tourists are as likely to swoon as locals when spotting Shah Rukh Khan in the queue for lunch at Olive Bar & Kitchen.

Then there's Mumbai's epic surge skywards. While downtown floats in a perpetual colonial summer, new towers are shooting up in the burbs faster than you can say Chowpatty Beach – more than 2500 at the latest count. Which is not to say there haven't been hiccups – intended to be India's tallest building, the India Tower at Girgaon stalled in a planning dispute, only be superseded by an even more ambitious scheme to build the world's tallest residential building at World One in Upper Worli.

Even arriving in Mumbai has been revitalised, with the creation of a gleaming new terminal at Chhatrapati Shivaji International Airport. People used to come to Mumbai for Raj relics and temples; now, it's all about food, shopping and movie tours.

Life-changing experience

The boat ride to Elephanta Island is more than a jaunt; it's a chance to flee the crowds, breathe some clean air, enjoy cooling sea breezes, and contemplate how colonialism came to Mumbai, and how it ended. Boats cast off beside the Gateway of India, where King George V arrived on his

Festivals & events

In September, thousands of vividly painted idols of the elephant-headed god Ganesh are paraded through the streets before a ceremonial dunking in the waters of Back Bay to celebrate Ganesh Chaturthi.

Every year brings more action to February's Kala Ghoda Festival, where cultured Mumbaikers enjoy drama, dance and art, before swanning off to dinner at some of the city's swankiest restaurants.

The home of Bollywood hosts the cream of film-making talent in October/November for the prestigious Mumbai Film Festival.

MUMBAI'S DHOBI GHAT LAUNDROMAT, WITH THE CITY SKYLINE BEYOND

first and only Indian tour, and where the last British soldiers on Indian soil performed one last parade before vacating the country in 1948. Colonialism even touched Elephanta, where some of the most dramatic temple carvings in India only narrowly escaped destruction at the hands of the Portuguese.

Current craze

Despite the monorail and an impending metro system, millions of Mumbaikars still depend on the city's congested suburban train network, and thrill seekers have made a sport out of performing stunts on the roofs of the unbelievably crowded carriages. It's insanely dangerous, and makes for compelling YouTube clips, with predictably tragic consequences

JOESBOY © GETTY IMAGES

Most bizarre sight

Hanging your dirty laundry out in public is de rigueur in Mumbai, where the city's dhobi-wallahs wash the city's laundry in the open air, in the sprawling ghats below the Mahalaxmi metro train station.

for many of the teenaged daredevils who risk life and limb in pursuit of the ultimate traintop selfie.

Trending topics

Mumbai lives by its stomach and food fads are front page news. When Bollywood superstar Aamir Khan turned vegan in 2015, millions were predicted to follow suit. Then there was the hashtag #beefban, retweeted by tens of thousands of Mumbaikars after the state government introduced a five-year jail term for the possession of beef. With more than a hint of the last days before Prohibition, prominent food bloggers created city tours of Bombay's best beef dishes to try before chefs purged their kitchens.

Classic place to stay

Founded by a Parsi industrialist who had had enough of being rejected by India's whites-only colonial hotels, the Taj Mahal Palace Hotel has been a Mumbai landmark for almost as long as there has been a Mumbai. Staying in this lavish cathedral of a hotel today, you'll see no evidence of the Taj's darkest hour, when militants stormed the historical old wing during citywide attacks in 2008. Instead, you can focus on the lush, East-meets-West interior, the ritzy restaurants and the hazy views across Mumbai harbour.

● *By Joe Bindloss*

A THRILLSEEKING
PERFORMER DRAWS THE
CROWDS AT FREO'S STREET
ART FESTIVAL

BEST IN
TRAVEL
2016

Fremantle, Australia

Under the baking Western Australian sun, Fremantle is a raffish harbour town with sea-salty soul to burn

CULTURE   EVENTS   FOOD

Population: **30,900**

Foreign visitors per year: **47,100**

Language: **English**

Unit of currency: **Australian dollar (A$)**

Cost index: **pint of craft beer A$10 (US$7.60), dorm bed per night A$28-33 (US$21-25), fish and chips dinner A$16 (US$12), spare change for a busker A$2 (US$1.50)**

7

Why go in 2016? > *Freo, way to go!*

Under the baking Western Australian sun, Fremantle is a raffish harbour town with sea-salty soul to burn. Like Valparaiso in Chile or Littleton in New Zealand, old-town 'Freo' is a tight nest of streets with a classic cache of Victorian and Edwardian buildings that somehow dodged the wrecking balls of the 1970s. It's an isolated place – closer to Jakarta than Sydney. But as in any port, the world washes in on the tide and washes out again, leaving the locals buzzing with global zeitgeist. It's a delicious process, and nowhere in Australia does it better. Fremantle thrums with live-music rooms, hipster bars, boutique hotels, left-field bookshops, craft-beer breweries, Indian Ocean seafood shacks, buskers, beaches and students on the run from the books.

A little context: Fremantle dragged itself out of the economic doldrums in 1987, scrubbing itself up to host the America's Cup yachting race. Once the yachties left town (the Americans taking the cup with them) the city faced the question of 'what now?'. A process of reinvention began, with investment in the arts, the establishment of Notre Dame University and the consolidation of the city's waterfront at the fore. In 2016, Freo is bearing the fruits of this process, with thriving urban culture and a string of awesome arts events celebrating the city's essence.

The city's cherished Australian Rules football team is also kicking goals this year. The Fremantle Dockers have played in the Australian Football League since 1995, but have only made the Grand Final once, losing narrowly to Hawthorn (from Melbourne) in 2013. But the Dockers just won't go away. They're one of the league's 'oldest' teams – a few Dockers are nudging retirement, including star captain Matthew Pavlich – but in 2016 they remain cherry-ripe for success. Get to Freo now see them boot some goals, take some big grabs and bust open some packs! Less convincing is the club's theme song... (Google it).

Life-changing experiences

Beer, students and Fremantle: it's all very simpatico. But a night spent mooching between the

Festivals & events

Over Easter, Freo's Street Arts Festival is one big busking party – more jugglers, mimes, musos and acrobats than loose change in your pocket. Fremantle actively fosters busking culture: charismatic Aussie guitar twanger John Butler got started here.

The Heritage Festival in May delivers a rootsy programme of talks, walking tours, exhibitions, music and theatre. Freo's gorgeous old Victorian and Edwardian architecture takes centre stage.

As high-brow as Freo gets, the Fremantle Festival in October/ November is the city's premier arts event, with Aboriginal culture, theatre, a street parade and kids' events aplenty.

MEZAIRI © SHUTTERSTOCK

pubs, breweries and bars here is about more than just beer. The Freo vibe is liberated, free-wheeling, engaging and infused with good music. Anonymous after dark on this forgotten rim of the planet, if you can't get a little perspective on life, love and longevity here there's something wrong. Essential booze rooms: Sail & Anchor, Little Creatures Brewery, Mrs Brown Bar.

Most bizarre sight

Legendary hell-raiser and AC/DC front man Bon Scott (1946–80) moved to Fremantle with his family in 1956. Bon spent his teen years strutting around Freo, and the city still adores him. Check out his statue down by Fishing Boat Harbour, in classic rock pose (more cock-sure than bizarre). His ashes are interred in Fremantle Cemetery: enter near the corner of High and Carrington Sts – Bon's plaque is 15m along the path on the left.

Classic restaurant experience

Fishing Boat Harbour is Fremantle's culinary crux: an arc of seafood eateries tracing the waterline, with something for all budgets. Kailis Fish Market Cafe has been cooking up fresh fish and chips here since 1986. Little Creatures Brewery continues to dazzle with zingy microbrews, hip staff and quick-fire eats in its lofty brew house. The food here is killer: order up a prawn, coriander pesto and shitake pizza, or a fiery chickpea tagine with goat's milk yoghurt.

Best shopping

Low-budget, spontaneous and surprising, MANY 6160 is a boho mashup of local artists' studios, pop-up shops and galleries on the ground floor of a defunct department store. A little more predictable are the Fremantle Markets, a hippie haven of craft stalls, buskers, coffee carts and produce vendors.

● *By Charles Rawlings-Way*

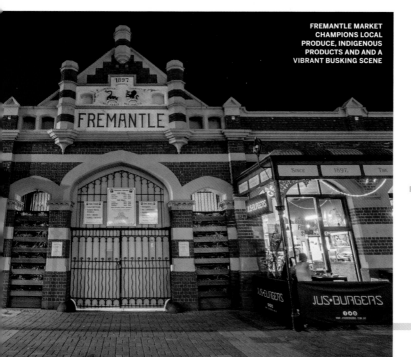

FREMANTLE MARKET CHAMPIONS LOCAL PRODUCE, INDIGENOUS PRODUCTS AND AND A VIBRANT BUSKING SCENE

What's hot...
Matthew Pavlich,
Fremantle Prison,
Little Creatures
Pale Ale

...What's not
Perth, the East Coast,
Victoria Bitter

BEST IN
TRAVEL
2016

SALFORD QUAYS IS THE
TEEMING HUB OF GREATER
MANCHESTER – COME
FOR CULTURE, SPORT
AND SHOPPING IN A
WATERFRONT SETTING

Manchester, UK

This one-time engine room of the Industrial Revolution has found a new groove for the 21st century as a dynamo of culture and the arts

CULTURE EVENTS FOOD

Population: **2.5 million**
Foreign visitors per year: **1.4 million**
Language: **English, with a pronounced Mancunian accent**
Unit of currency: **pound sterling (£)**
Cost index: **pint of beer £3.10 (US$4.60), hotel double/dorm bed per night £65-120 (US$96-180)/£14-20 (US$20-30), short taxi ride £6 (US$9), admission to live-music gig £6-15 (US$9-22)**

8

Why go in 2016? › The UK's cultural boomtown

Raised on lofty ambition and never afraid to declare its considerable bona fides, the one-time engine room of the Industrial Revolution has found a new groove for the 21st century as a dynamo of culture and the arts. And the government agrees: it has committed £78m to build The Factory, a new, multi-purpose arts space that will include a 2200 theatre and will be the permanent home of the Manchester International Festival.

One of Britain's most important art galleries, the Whitworth, reopened in 2015 after a £15 million revamp with a new glass promenade and art

CHRIS HEPBURN © GETTY IMAGES

garden. A few months later saw the opening of HOME, a multi-artform centre with ambitions to produce the country's best theatre, film and visual art. Britain's second largest public library, the pantheon-like Central Library, reopened in 2014 as a 'living-room space' for the city, with a media lounge, British Film Institute Mediatheque, music library and a modern children's library to boot.

Injecting fun into culture is the new Breakout on Brazennose St, a 'real-life escape room game' based on puzzle game shows like *The Krypton Factor*, where participants gather clues and hints to crack the lock on the escape door. And 17 years after the city served as the setting for Russell T Davies' ground-breaking gay TV drama *Queer as Folk*, Manchester is once again the backdrop for Davies' newest endeavour, the frank and very funny *Cucumber*.

Life-changing experiences

■ Get to the heart of the city's most divisive passion and take in a match at either Old Trafford, home to one of the

What's hot...
Multimeda, football, local artisans

...What's not
Madchester, chain bars, Chelsea Football Club

MANCHESTER'S NEWLY RESTORED CENTRAL LIBRARY WAS OPENED BY GEORGE V IN 1934

BEST IN TRAVEL 2016

world's most popular football clubs, Manchester United, or the Etihad Stadium, where recently cashed-up football powerhouse Manchester City stake their claim to be the city's finest.

■ Hop on a Saturday suburban train to south Manchester and immerse yourself in the community-minded Levenshulme Market, the city's best for food, artisanal wares and a host of other locally made goodies (March to December only).

■ Go the distance in the all-night Islington Mill, a multi-purpose venue in Salford where you can sweat to everything from Bikram yoga to hardcore techno.

Most bizarre sight

Dominating the skyline of north Manchester is the 71m ventilation tower of Strangeways Prison, the city's main detention centre, which is featured in the title of The Smiths' album *Strangeways, Here We Come*. Many people mistakenly think it's an over-tall guard tower, but everyone agrees that its height serves as a constant reminder to the city that crime doesn't pay.

Classic restaurant experience

Manchester has no shortage of fine dining, but since opening in 2013 Manchester House delivers it with plenty of local flair. Inspired by the molecular gastronomy of Blumenthal and El Bulli, chef Aiden Byrne serves up carefully crafted delicacies that have all of the sophistication but none of the preciousness of haute cuisine. The dining room is all industrial chic and informal elegance; even more popular is the buzzy lounge on the 12th floor, with its cocktails and local brews, to be enjoyed with stunning views of the Manchester cityscape.

Best shopping

From the boutiques of South King St and the high-fashion stores of Spinningfields to the high-street cornucopia of the Arndale Centre and the hipster shops of the Northern Quarter, Manchester has a cure for every strain of retail fever. One of the most interesting openings has been the Manchester Craft & Design Centre in a converted Victorian fish market on Oak St in the Northern Quarter. Here you can buy jewellery, ceramics, textiles and clothing made by the 30-odd designers in situ.

Classic place to stay

Great John Street Hotel. Elegant designer luxury? Present. Hotel delights – Egyptian cotton sheets, luxe toiletries, free-standing baths and lots of high-tech electronics? Present. This former schoolhouse (ah, now you get it) is small but sumptuous – beyond the Art Deco lobby are the fabulous bedrooms, each an example of style and luxury. If only school left such comfortable memories. ● *By Fionn Davenport*

Festivals & events

Manchester is European City of Science in 2016 – the theme of late July's EuroScience Open Forum is what the city was built on: breakthroughs in science and the conditions needed for a city to capitalise on scientific knowledge (it's way more interesting than it sounds!).

Manchester Pride's main event is the Big Weekend at the end of August, and it's immediately preceded by a month-long fringe festival of arts, culture, music and comedy.

The city's gourmet credentials and craft beer revolution are celebrated during the Manchester Food and Drink Festival, which takes place over 10 days in September.

COUNTRY MUSIC RUNS IN THE BLOOD IN NASHVILLE, THE SELF-STYLED 'MUSIC CITY'

BEST IN
TRAVEL
2016

Nashville, USA

While crooners downtown may sing of ruin and raising hell, tastemakers are busy opening hip breweries, coffee roasters and independent fashion stores

CULTURE | EVENTS | FOOD

Population: **1.7 million**
Foreign visitors per year: **900,000**
Language: **English, with a southern drawl**
Unit of currency: **US dollar (US$)**
Cost index: **glass of Yazoo pale ale US$5, hotel double for a night US$70-300, short Uber cab ride US$5, concert at the Ryman Auditorium US$30-130, depending on the artist, pair of cowboy boots from Boots Country US$95-700, depending on the boot**

→ **Why go in 2016?**
> *Hotter (and sproutier) than a pepper sprout*

If you thought Nashville was all about twanging guitars, big hair and cheatin' hearts, well, you'd be right. Country is still the heart and soul of Music City, and with the likes of Taylor Swift hitting the global big time, this once vaguely uncool scene is as vibrant and popular is it ever was. Poke your head outside the honky tonks of lower Broadway, however, and you'll notice new sounds in the air: the grind of construction work, excited chatter at the latest restaurant or art gallery opening and, loudest of all, the energetic thrum of new business. Nashville is experiencing an extended period of growth, and is a shining example of the US economic recovery at full, gentrifying, pelt. Hordes of young people are moving to town as much for the music and friendly Southern ways as for job opportunities and a low cost of living. With booming tech, healthcare and automotive industries, Nashville was chosen as one of the seven US cities to begin the Google for Entrepreneurs Tech Hub Network, and has become a veritable petri dish for start-ups.

Times are good in Nashville and the spoils are there for the taking. While crooners downtown may sing of ruin and raising hell, tastemakers are busy opening hip breweries, coffee roasters and independent fashion stores or transforming once-abandoned warehouses into creative retail space.

Trendy brands such as Eventbrite, Warby Parker, and (ahem) Lonely Planet have all recently opened offices here and filmmakers, designers and other creative types are flooding in to see what all the fuss is about. The dining scene in particular is unrecognisable: while carnivores shouldn't miss the region's signature barbecue and 'meat and three', celebrated chefs and food talent are bringing a sleeker brand of eatery to town. Rolf & Daughters, Husk Nashville, and Catbird Seat have all been listed as some of the country's finest new restaurants. Just make sure you reserve well in advance.

Festivals & events

For five days at the end of March around 350 songwriters perform original work for the Tin Pan South Songwriters Festival. It's one of the largest events of its kind in the world.

Thousands of cowboy hat-wearing country fans arrive in June for the four-day CMA Music Festival when the best in the genre play at their spiritual home.

Only in its fourth year, the Music City Food + Wine Festival showcases the best eats and drinks in town and beyond. Top chefs give talks, demos and tastings over two days in September. There's also live music (of course) by the likes of co-founders Kings of Leon, among others.

Life-changing experiences

Music pilgrims will be in seventh heaven: on the surprisingly low-key Music Row you can tour the recording studio where Dolly and Elvis cut their hits, before heading down to Jack White's Third Man Records to pick up some vinyl for yourself. If you can get a ticket, the live shows here are legendary: the Blue Room is the only venue in the world to record direct-to-acetate during a performance. For the full Grand Ole Opry experience, the Ryman Auditorium is known as the 'Mother Church' of country music with acoustics that may well transport you to spiritual realms.

Current craze

Hand-stitched neck ties from Otis James, Brambleberry Crisp ice cream from Jeni's, Emil Erwin leather belts, gourmet Mexican ice lollies, hand-blended tea... If it's artisan and specialist, it's here.

ON THE OUTSKIRTS OF NASHVILLE, THE LOVELESS CAFE HAS BEEN SERVING UP FRIED CHICKEN AND BISCUITS FOR MORE THAN 60 YEARS

Trending topic
Google Fiber. The fiber is coming, although when the next-generation super-speedy internet will be available is frustratingly mysterious.

Random facts
■ The world's only full-scale replica of the Parthenon in Athens sits in Nashville's Centennial Park.
■ As legend has it, Roy Orbison's hit 'Oh, Pretty Woman' was inspired as he was looking out of his 8th Avenue apartment and saw a lovely lady.
■ Printers Alley first became a nightlife hub when men from the printing houses would hang around on the street during a print run.

Most bizarre sight
The Lane Motor Museum displays an A to Z of fabulous vehicular oddities, including the largest collection of Czechoslovakian cars outside Europe and the world's smallest production automobile. Bubble cars, micro cars, wooden cars, propeller cars and amphibious cars: it's a petrol nerd's dream. A to Z? That's Amphicar to Zündapp.

Classic restaurant experience
Legend has it that Nashville's most famous gift to the culinary world was an act of revenge. When serial womaniser Thornton Prince returned home later than usual one night his girlfriend at the time gave his breakfast fried chicken an extra dousing of hot pepper. It didn't pay off as Prince liked the chicken so much he opened a restaurant dedicated to it. Prince's Hot Chicken Shack has been serving up succulent spicy chicken and pickle sandwiches to the Nashville great and good ever since. It's a no-frills must. ● *By Dora Whitaker*

THE RESTORATION OF THE
COLOSSEUM WILL LEAVE IT
FRESHLY GLEAMING FOR
VISITORS IN 2016

BEST IN
TRAVEL
2016

Rome, Italy

There's magic on every corner of Rome, with its sunbaked piazzas, ancient splendour, masterpiece-packed churches, and Vespa-whizzing Italian style

CULTURE | EVENTS | FOOD

Population: **3.3 million**
Foreign visitors per year: **8.6 million**
Language: **Italian**
Unit of currency: **euro (€)**
Cost index: **cup of coffee €1 (US$1.10), glass of beer or wine €5 (US$5.50), hotel double/dorm room for a night from €80/30 (US$88/33), margherita pizza €5 (US$5.50), ice cream cone from €2.50 (US$2.75)**

Why go in 2016? > *Shiny, happy city*

Rome is a capital with charisma. There's magic on every corner, with its sunbaked piazzas, ancient splendour, masterpiece-packed churches, and Vespa-whizzing Italian style. But 2016 is a particularly sublime time to visit. It's an official global jubilee Year of Mercy, as announced by Pope Francis last year, attracting streams of pilgrims to the city to celebrate their faith. But it's also a great year in more earthly terms, as the Colosseum's huge-scale restoration job is finally being unveiled.

Having spent several years under wraps, the ancient Roman stadium is finally exposed in all its scrubbed-up splendour. In 2013, the Italian Ministry of Culture and Tourism partnered with luxury leather-goods company Tod's, which donated €25 million to fund the spit and polish. Gladiatorial armies of archaeologists and cleaners have since carefully worked on cleaning the 2000-year-old building using nebulised water.

Likewise the Trevi Fountain is this year revealed in its full, foaming glory, following a major clean funded by luxury label Fendi, which also funded the cleaning of four other major fountains. Not for centuries have Rome's major monuments looked so radiant.

But that's not all. This year also sees a Roman feast of cinematic treats.

Imagine yourself back in ancient Rome, cheering the chariots around the Circo Massimo (Circus Maximus), as the remake of *Ben Hur* hits the big screen. When in Rome you can visit Cinecittà, the famous film studios built by Mussolini, and see where some of the film's scenes were created. The latest James Bond, *Spectre*, is partly set in Rome, featuring thrilling car chases along the River Tiber. If you need any inspiration to hit Rome's streets, current bombastic blockbusters have it in spades.

Life-changing experiences

Gaze over the ochre cityscape from one of Rome's many viewpoints, counting the domes that rise like islands from this higgeldy-piggeldy city of gold. Amble past some of the world's most beautiful architecture, eating some of the world's best ice

What's hot...
Sunglasses, even when it's not so sunny.

What's not...
Flip flops on city streets. Casual beach wear is confined to the beach, unless you want to out yourself as an unstylish foreigner. Also a cappuccino after 11am: milky coffee in the afternoon? You must be *pazzo/a* (crazy) or a *straniero/a* (foreigner).

TRASTAVERE, FORMERLY A WORKING-CLASS DISTRICT, NOW OFFERS CAFE-PEPPERED LANES AND A HEADY NIGHTLIFE

CATARINA BELOVA © SHUTTERSTOCK

BEST IN TRAVEL 2016

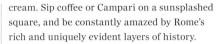

> **Amble past some of the world's most beautiful architecture, eating some of the world's best ice cream**

Festivals & events

The Year of Mercy concludes on 20 November, on the Feast of Christ the King.

The International Choral Festival (22-26 June) hosts choral masses at St Peter's, and has a grand finale at the Basilica of Saint Mary above Minerva, under a blue ceiling spangled with gilded stars.

The Teatro dell'Opera di Roma is most spectacular when it takes the music outside in June and July, with magnificent opera and ballet productions on sultry nights against the backdrop of the Terme di Caracalla, epic ruined Roman baths.

cream. Sip coffee or Campari on a sunsplashed square, and be constantly amazed by Rome's rich and uniquely evident layers of history.

Current craze

Local hawkers have ditched selling spinning light-up things, and presently provide a forest of selfie sticks at every tourist hotspot. But, as if by magic, they're always handily proffering umbrellas for sale whenever it rains (which is rare).

Trending topic

Will the current municipal government maintain Rome as it deserves? The previous administration has been tainted by the discovery of endemic corruption, whereby prominent figures embezzled money intended for the city's upkeep and services.

Most bizarre sight

A toss-up between the Museum of the Souls of Purgatory (Museo delle Anime dei Defunti; Lungotevere Prati 12), devoted to lost souls who linger in the netherworld and displaying scorched handprints on prayer books and the like, and the Capuchin Crypt at Santa Maria della Concezione dei Cappuccini (Via Veneto), with a row of subterranean chapels completely decorated with human bones.

Best shopping

If you can tear yourself away from the sights, romantic wandering, and cuisine, Rome is a wonderful place to shop, with lots of independent boutiques selling enticing wares such as hand-made scents or hand-painted paper. However, the most wonderful thing about shopping in Rome is its artisans. In backstreet dusty workshops, people work on making picture frames or sewing leather goods, and you can commission bespoke leather goods or an engraved marble tablet.

● *By Abigail Blasi*

Lonely Planet's
Top travel lists

Best value destinations

Our essential annual hot-list of where in the world to go for wallet-friendly wandering, whether you're hunting for a bargain or in search of old-school cheapness. Splurgers, look elsewhere.

HANOI'S STREETS
BUSTLE WITH LIFE

BEST IN
TRAVEL
2016

1 Estonia

If you've just got off the ferry from Stockholm or Helsinki then Estonia can feel like the promised land. Why? That chunk of change in your pocket you've had since last leaving the eurozone will buy you a round of drinks. Upsizing from a hostel to hotel might seem like a good – and affordable – idea. Best of all, what you get in exchange for your hard-earned cash is experiencing a gloriously distinctive slice of Europe, where Eastern and Nordic influences mix together. Beyond the irresistible capital of Tallinn there are little-known Baltic islands and the seashore and forest delights of Lahemaa National Park, which holds the distinction of being the first national park in the old Soviet Union.

The most cost-effective way to reach Estonia is to take a low-cost flight from a European hub. Shop around: Skyscanner (www.skyscanner.net) is a good place to look for fares from a multitude of carriers.

2 Ho Chi Minh City & Hanoi, Vietnam

The Price of Travel's Backpacker Index (www. priceoftravel.com), ranking 31 Asian cities by price, confirms what many travellers have known for a while – Vietnam's cities are tops for budget options. Both Ho Chi Minh City and Hanoi (second and third in the list respectively) are in that most magical of price brackets for the budget traveller: US$20 per day or less for food, lodging and sights. Finding these prices will take you firmly into the territory of living like a local, which is another vote in favour of making a super-cheap city trip at some point this year.

Bia hoi, Vietnam's famously low-priced beer, can be had for a few cents a glass across the country. You'll need a few to get any buzz, and quality varies, but you can afford to try a few. Every day.

3 East Africa

The outbreak of the Ebola virus in West Africa has, unfortunately for other areas of the continent, had a knock-on effect in terms of bookings for 2015. So listen up: London, Madrid and Paris are hundreds of miles closer to the outbreak in West Africa than East Africa's tourism heartland. Africa is a massive continent (the United States would fit in the Sahara Desert), so you'll be doing yourself and tourism in East Africa a favour if you take advantage of the cracking deals on offer to Kenya, Uganda, Tanzania and the rest of the region. And in the process experience some of the world's great wonders, from gorilla encounters to Rift Valley scenery to squeaky-sanded beaches.

Explore Africa has a blog post offering Ebola information, perspective and a sobering geography lesson: www.exploreafrica.net/news/no-you-wont-catch-ebola-from-a-giraffe-in-kenya.

4 New Mexico, USA

Looking for a beautiful, affordable, active, foodie corner of America's southwest? Look no further. New Mexico powers your budget further. Dry, sunny weather is a near constant. Albuquerque's *Breaking Bad* sights can be explored for the price of a trolley ride and washed down with a cheap eat from a hole-in-the-wall taqueria. Elsewhere, the winter sports are good and cheap and the outdoors is outstanding (and free): hiking in Alpine forests, petroglyph sites to track down and free wild hot springs. Given the richness of attractions all found within one state, New Mexico offers value from a time as well as monetary perspective.

For deals, coupons and bargains see the New Mexico website: newmexico. org/deals.

5 Bosnia & Hercegovina

All it takes to make Europe's big hitters feel very pricey is for a few currency fluctuations to work against you. Thankfully there are still a few places where regardless of where you come from you'll feel like you're getting a good deal. Bosnia and Hercegovina is one of those. Inexpensive accommodation, meals and intercity transport combined with historic cities (Sarajevo and Mostar) and affordable adrenaline pursuits (rafting on the Una River and skiing) reward both the impecunious and those seeking a less well-travelled Europe.

Bosnia and Hercegovina can easily be combined with Balkan neighbours. Buses are the easiest way to get around.

6 Galicia, Spain

Spain. Mapped by travellers? Not completely. Galicia in the northwest of the country is arguably Spain's last frontier. Once you get beyond Santiago de Compostela, this wild region fragments into rocky coastline met by spectacular *rías* (inlets) and an interior of countless unspoilt villages. The region's value comes not only from the lower costs compared with more-visited parts of Spain, but also from the quality of seafood and meat found in abundance in tapas bars, meaning tasting the good stuff in small portions costs less. And if you're keen to save while sleeping over, aim for self-catering properties around the region, especially outside the school holidays.

Santiago gets the lion's share of flights into the region, but Vigo and A Coruña are also affordable gateways to Galicia from around Europe.

7 Québec City, Canada

What to do if you live in North America and want to visit Europe, but lack the time and funds? Consider Québec City. Yes, we know it's not in Europe. But there's enough of the exotic in this Francophone city to remind you of the Old Continent. In a few days you can tour the beautiful, Unesco-listed old town, dine in old-school bistros and get thoroughly lost in the timeless cobblestone streets. With a little more time and your own wheels, Montmorency Forest and Jacques-Cartier National Park offer a wilder taste of the province and superb wildlife-viewing opportunities surprisingly close to the city.

Québec's annual Winter Carnival (29 January to 14 February) is a hugely exciting cold-weather event. You'll find parades, ice sculptures and outdoor winter sports events and banquets.

8 Costa Rica's Caribbean coast

Looking for a Costa Rica that's more Tico than

tourist, but with everything that makes the country such a big draw? Get to the country's Caribbean coast and you'll find a still-evolving destination that's likely to become a big noise over the next few years. Here you'll find nesting turtles at Tortuguero, rafting on the Río Pacuare and diving in the reefs of Manzanillo. Surfers and fans of laid-back black-sand beaches should aim for the southern coast. For now, this is a land mostly visited by independent travellers and those seeking out birdlife. Not sold? Two words: sloth sanctuary.

A wise investment for wildlife spotters is a good set of binoculars. They are easier to source from overseas, and they transform rainforest walks into bird-spotting adventures.

9 Timor-Leste

If you're pondering a little-known and highly affordable destination then Timor-Leste (rather than East Timor, if you please) might just be the budget destination for you. Away from the pricey hotels of the internationally-influenced capital of Dili, you'll find bargain beach shacks on the pristine beaches of Jaco and Atauro Islands plus misty hill country and affordable guest houses. Despite ongoing security concerns, travelling round Timor can be an old-fashioned adventure, complete with bumpy roads and packed local transport. As an added bonus, you will be able to stare down any travel bore with Asia's newest country added to your roster.

The most expensive part of a trip to Timor is likely to be the airfare. You can reach Dili from Darwin, Denpasar and Singapore. Book early for the best fares.

10 Western Australia

Currency fluctuations mean that the Australian dollar is a better deal for overseas visitors than it has been for a few years, and that Aussies may scale back overseas plans. This puts the dream-like landscapes of Western Australia, out of reach of some travellers thanks to the mining boom of the last few years, firmly back on the map. Beyond cosmopolitan Perth, iconic natural sights abound here, from the rocky coast and winelands of the southwest to the outback treats of the Kimberley, Kununurra and the Pinnacles.

Perth's premier cultural institutions are free, so wallet-friendly exploring can be had at the Western Australian Museum, Art Gallery of Western Australia, State Library of Western Australia and Perth Institute of Contemporary Arts. ● *By Tom Hall*

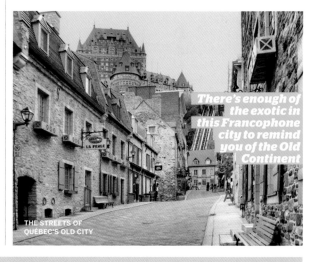

There's enough of the exotic in this Francophone city to remind you of the Old Continent

THE STREETS OF QUÉBEC'S OLD CITY

Best new openings

Be the first kid on your block to see these brand new attractions, all slated to throw open their doors by 2016.

1 Monnaie de Paris, France

Mid-2016 sees the French capital's 18th-century royal mint reach the completion of its 'MetaLmorphoses' project – a multiphased transformation of its monumental 1.2-hectare site on the Seine's Left Bank. Following 2014's contemporary art exhibitions in the mint's sumptuous neoclassical building and the 2015 arrival of triple-Michelin-starred chef Guy Savoy's flagship restaurant, 2016 will unveil the Monnaie de Paris' previously unseen collections. Along with these will be metalwork and foundry workshop tours, boutiques, Guy Savoy's MetaLcafé brasserie, and interior streets and a park overlooked by a restored 1690 town house built by Jules Hardouin Mansart, publicly viewable for the first time.
The Monnaie de Paris is located at 11 quai de Conti, 6th arrondissement (metro Pont Neuf). See www.monnaiedeparis.fr.

2 Shanghai Disney Resort, China

Slated to open in spring 2016, Disney's newest resort – and its first in mainland China – will feature a traditional Magic Kingdom park complete with the largest-yet Enchanted Storybook Castle. Rides and attractions will be scattered around six themed lands, including the pirate-themed Treasure Cove with the high-tech Pirates of the Caribbean: Battle of the Sunken Treasure ride. The Garden of the Twelve Friends at the park's centre will contain murals of the 12 animals of the Chinese zodiac depicted as Disney characters. Just outside the Magic Kingdom, the Disneytown entertainment district will have restaurants, shopping and nightlife, including a theatre showing a Mandarin-language version of

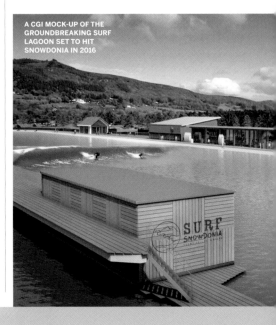

A CGI MOCK-UP OF THE GROUNDBREAKING SURF LAGOON SET TO HIT SNOWDONIA IN 2016

The Lion King. Two hotels, the Art Nouveau–style Shanghai Disneyland Hotel and the Toy Story Hotel, will accommodate guests in the park. *Shanghai Disney is located in Pudong in southeastern Shanghai. An extension of metro line 11 will go to a dedicated Disney Resort station, and the Maglev train to Pudong airport will also connect to the park.*

3 Louvre Abu Dhabi, UAE

In true Gulf style, the Louvre Abu Dhabi is magnificently ambitious on every level. The futuristic, dome-shaped building is an architectural feat in itself, appearing to float above a man-made lake. Permanent collections will represent art throughout the ages, including everything from Chinese Buddhist carvings to Italian oil paintings, while France's most renowned art institutes are to lend Abu Dhabi 300 additional works – Van Gogh, Monet and da Vinci masterpieces among their number. Louvre Abu Dhabi's development has involved plenty of controversies. But finally opening in 2016, it has the potential to rival the world's greatest art museums and be a real cultural game-changer for the Middle East.

The Louvre is part of a cultural district in the making on Abu Dhabi's Saadiyat Island.

4 Mamma Mia! The Party, Stockholm, Sweden

Take one part restaurant, one part performance, a generous splash of disco, a touch of audience participation and what do you get? A new *Mamma Mia!*–themed restaurant, slated to open in Stockholm's Gröna Lund amusement park in January 2016. ABBA legend Björn Ulvaeus is behind the new interactive disco-dining experience, a Greek-style taverna where diners tuck into souvlaki while a story unfolds around them. With the chance to take part in the show, and to sing and dance to the hits featured in the world-famous musical, it's set to be a delicious feast of ABBA fun.

Gröna Lund is easily reached by tram (7), bus (44) or ferry (Slussen–Djurgården route). Keep up-to-date with plans at www. mammamiatheparty.com.

Top travel lists ● ● ● ● ● ● ●
● ● ● ● ● ● ● ●

5 FIFA World Football Museum, Zurich, Switzerland

Zurich is upping its game as it braces itself to welcome the new FIFA World Football Museum, slated to open in spring 2016 and costing a cool Sfr180 million. It's the moment footie fans have been waiting for with bated breath. Bang in the heart of the city, the 3500-sq-metre whopper of a museum will whisk fans through the history of the game, with a timeline, hall of fame and cinema; recreate stadium fever with a giant football pinball machine; and harbour the world's biggest collection of football books. Huddled away in the basement is the museum's very own *Mona Lisa:* the World Cup Trophy itself.

Situated in the Enge quarter, the museum will be a 17-minute ride on trams 7 and 13 or a five-minute journey by train from the Hauptbahnhof. Single tickets cost Sfr4.30.

6 Surf Snowdonia, Wales

The magical mountains and valleys of Snowdonia are a great place for walkers and adventure sports fans. The natural landscape is increasingly being augmented by impressive man-made facilities – Snowdonia now boasts Europe's longest zip line and a vast underground trampolining centre. But its most radical attraction will have been freshly opened come 2016: a £12 million, 300m-long artificial surf lagoon that uses local rainwater to produce a consistent, barrelling 2m wave every sixty seconds. It's a world first, and one that doesn't just appeal to the hardcore – the wave's size varies in different parts of the lagoon, and its consistency helps beginners. Surf kayaking, stand up paddle boarding and blobbing are also on offer.

Surf Snowdonia in situated in Dolgarrog, North Wales. See http://surfsnowdonia.co.uk for more.

7 Bourdain Market, New York City, USA

Really good chicken rice, giant sexy robots and chaos: we don't know a huge amount about what will feature in the Bourdain Market when it opens in early 2016, but what has been revealed is tantalizing stuff. Chef, food writer and mischievous gastronomic explorer Anthony Bourdain announced his plan to open an NYC-based international food market back in January 2014, and the food press has been salivating over every tiny detail ever since. The market will cover a massive 100,000 sq ft of space and will comprise around 100 carefully selected chefs, producers and street food talent from around the globe in a big bustling hawker center-style food hall on Pier 57. Although many details are still an unknown, the design for the space is going to be 'crazy-looking' and inspired by Blade Runner. If that's not enough to whet your appetite, there will also be a butchery, a farmers' market, a rooftop beer garden and an oyster bar.

At the time of writing details are few and far between, but follow @Bourdain on Twitter for the latest updates as the project develops.

8 National Gallery Singapore

Singapore boasts several world-class museums, but if you only have time to see one in 2016, make it the National Gallery Singapore. Occupying two of central Singapore's most historical buildings – the former City Hall and Supreme Court – the enormous gallery space, unveiled during the city-state's 50th birthday celebrations in November 2015, will showcase Southeast Asian art from the 19th century to the present day. After admiring the thousand-odd artworks in the painstakingly restored colonial courtrooms and council chambers, don't miss the fifth-floor rooftop garden with its superb views across the Padang towards Marina Bay. *The National Gallery Singapore is located at 1 St Andrew's Road. For information, visit nationalgallery.sg.*

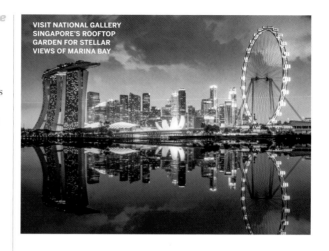

VISIT NATIONAL GALLERY SINGAPORE'S ROOFTOP GARDEN FOR STELLAR VIEWS OF MARINA BAY

9 BASK, Gili Meno, Indonesia

You might think you'd be more likely to bump into David Hasselhoff at a German karaoke bar, but if you're headed to Indonesia you might just see him by the pool. For The Hoff is the face of BASK, a luxury villa-resort development currently under construction on Gili Meno, near Bali. Situated on a private white-sand beach, BASK will boast a world-class restaurant, chic beach club, state-of-the-art spa and its very own underwater sculpture park. Not to mention a star in its midst – the entertainer is said to be eyeing off a three-bedroom 'Hoff Hideaway' vacation villa of his own here. *Located on the western shore of Gili Meno, accessible by boat from Bali (via Gili Trawangan), BASK is due to open in early 2016. For info and villa sales, visit baskgilimeno.com.*

10 National Museum of African American History and Culture, Washington, DC, USA

On its inauguration the NMAAHC will become America's first national museum devoted exclusively to African American life, history and culture. The 10-storey space will house artefacts from all over the country and history – from Harriet Tubman's 1876 hymn book, to a Jim Crow-era segregated railcar, to banners and photographs from the #BlackLivesMatter demonstrations. *Although running behind schedule, the museum will open before November 2016 – the ribbon will be cut by Barack Obama, while he is still president.*
● *By Lonely Planet's Destination Editors*

Top travel lists

Special anniversaries in 2016

Great writers. Great novels. Celebrations of nature and commemorations of war. Movie world glamour and national independence. The anniversaries taking place in 2016 form an eclectic group.

1 400 years since Shakespeare died, England

The greatest and best-known writer in the English language, William Shakespeare, is commonly said to have died on 23 April in 1616. Actor, playwright and poet, his talents placed him at the centre of the extraordinary golden age of literature that flourished in England in the late 1500s/early 1600s. During a relatively short life (he died in his early 50s) his output was impressive – about 38 plays (the number is disputed), 154 sonnets and innumerable quotable quotes – leaving a legacy that is as popular today as it was 400 years ago. *Seeing a production at Shakespeare's Globe in London or the Swan Theatre in Shakespeare's home town, Stratford-upon-Avon, is a perfect way of understanding his enduring popularity. Details*

YELLOWSTONE RIVER
WENDS ITS WAY THROUGH
HAYDEN VALLEY

of worldwide celebrations marking the anniversary can be found at www.stahome.org.

2 80 years since start of the Spanish Civil War, Spain

When the Spanish Civil War broke out in July 1936 it was immediately recognised as a struggle that reflected the political divisions across the whole of Europe at the time. A group of generals, led by future dictator Franco and backed by right-wing factions, revolted against the newly elected left-wing government, beginning a bitter struggle that lasted almost three years and ended in a fascist victory. The aerial bombings and mass civilian casualties of the Spanish Civil War presaged the horrors of WWII which began just months after the fighting in Spain finished.

See Picasso's painting Guernica *in the Reina Sofía Museum in Madrid. It's a moving depiction of the destruction of a small Basque town by German bombers in 1937.*

3 50 years of independence for Botswana

In the history of post-colonial Africa, Botswana is a success story. The transition from British-controlled Bechuanaland to independent Botswana in September 1966 was done peacefully, and in the half-century since then the country has remained a stable democracy in a continent often plagued by political insecurity. The country's diversity of landscapes (Kalahari Desert, Okavango Delta) and rich wildlife (the Big Five can all be seen here) have made it a prime destination for travellers who want to enjoy the full African experience.

For information on visiting Botswana and being part of the 50th anniversary celebrations go to www.botswanatourism.co.bw.

4 100 years of the National Park Service, USA

These days we've become used to the idea of protecting our most beautiful natural environments, but just a hundred years ago the principle was less developed. After a piecemeal approach in the 19th century, spearheaded by iconic figures such as John Muir, the US federal government decided in 1916 to create an independent body to oversee the country's most precious landscapes and monuments. The National Park Service (NPS) was born and today continues to look after and promote the 59 parks under its control.

Visit www.nps.gov to see what the NPS has lined up for its centenary.

5 The Cannes Film Festival turns 70, France

For glitz and glamour no other film festival has the appeal of Cannes. A popular holiday destination for wealthy British and American travellers since the late 19th century, the fortunes of this chic French resort became irreversibly linked with the movie world in 1946 when the first festival was held. Ever since, directors, actors, screenwriters and anyone in the film world have hoped to be asked to show their work at the invite-only event in May each year.

Booking well in advance is necessary. Start planning at www.cannes-destination.com.

Top travel lists ● ● ● ● ● ● ● ● ● ● ● ● ● ● ● ● ●

6 Frankenstein was born 200 years ago, Switzerland

When bad weather ruins your vacation what do you do? If you're Mary Shelley you dream up the idea for one of the most enduring horror stories ever written, *Frankenstein*. When she and a group of friends, including Lord Byron, were holed up in Villa Diodati in Switzerland during the terrible summer of 1816, they challenged each other to come up with the best tale of terror. Shelley invented the story of Frankenstein (the name of the doctor, not the monster) and the creature he brings to life, and a legend was born.

Villa Diodati is private property and can't be visited, but much of the book is set in and around Geneva, which offers plenty to explore. See www.geneve-tourisme.ch for details.

7 50 years after the floods, Florence, Italy

For centuries Florence has been known as a centre of art and culture with world-famous museums and monuments. For two days in November 1966, however, it was known for a devastating flood that left over a hundred people dead and thousands of works of art damaged. Water levels in the River Arno started rising after days of heavy rain until on 3 November it burst its banks and inundated the city, rising up to 6.7m in places. The devastation was huge and work still goes on today repairing some of the damage done. *The website www.florence-flood.com has much more information on the events of 1966. To find out more about visiting the city today go to www.visitflorence.com.*

8 350 years since the Great Fire of London, England

The Great Fire of London began on 2 September 1666 and burned for four days. Caused by an accident in a bakery (though at the time everything from Catholics to the greed of London's citizens were blamed), the fire was one of the biggest disasters and also greatest opportunities in the city's history. It destroyed the old St Paul's Cathedral and around 13,200 homes, and killed at least six people (though it's thought more might have died and been burnt beyond recognition). Yet out of this catastrophe grew a modern city, built of non-flammable brick and stone rather than wood, a city that would never again be visited by the plague and would soon be the heart of a globe-spanning empire.

The Museum of London (www.museumoflondon.org.uk) has a whole section dedicated to the Great Fire. For a view over the city that rose from the fire's ashes, climb the Monument (www.themonument.info), built to commemorate the event.

9 Centenary of the Easter Rising, Dublin, Ireland

1916 saw the political struggle for independence in Ireland turn violent. On Easter Monday Irish Republicans took control of strategic locations across Dublin and, from their headquarters at the city's General Post Office, proclaimed an independent Ireland, hoping to end British rule. Taken by surprise, the British soon responded with overwhelming force and within six days it was all over, leaving hundreds dead, including many civilians, and large areas of the city destroyed. Dubliners' fury was initially aimed at the rebels who were jeered as they were arrested, but when Britain, struggling in World War I, began to execute those involved in the rising for treason, opinion changed, creating an unstoppable momentum that led to independence within a few years.

The General Post Office (www.anpost.ie/AnPost/History+and+Heritage/Museum) on O'Connell St has an exhibition on the building and its role in the Easter Rising.

10 75 years since the attack on Pearl Harbor, USA

When World War II began in 1939, the prospect of joining yet another bloody conflict was an unpopular one in the US. But on 7 December 1941, Japanese forces launched a surprise attack on the US Pacific Fleet, anchored in the Hawaiian port of Pearl Harbor, and by the end of that 'date which will live in infamy', as President Roosevelt called it, thousands of Americans, both military personnel and civilians, were dead and the country was ready to join the fight.

Honolulu's Pearl Harbor Visitor Center is operated by the National Park Service. For more information see www.nps.gov/valr.

● *By Cliff Wilkinson*

Best animal adventures for families

Furry, feathered or fishy? Whatever your preference, children and adults alike will be fascinated by these amazing opportunities to see different creatures at play.

1 Giant Panda Breeding Research Base, Chengdu, China

See the doe-eyed balls of black-and-white fluff in the most natural environment possible at this research centre which was established in 1987 to rescue and protect the endangered panda. The animals roam around their large, carefully landscaped enclosures and can watch these beautiful beasts at play, at rest, sleeping and eating. Come early in the morning to see the baby pandas at their best. Note, there is an option to 'hug a panda'. Whether the panda enjoys this experience is debatable, so best think ahead about this choice. *Plan your visit at www.panda.org. cn. Use the park's shuttle bus to get around the park to keep little legs full of beans. Talk to your kids ahead* of your visit to make sure they understand why they need to be quiet while there.

2 Galápagos Islands, Ecuador

Surely the ultimate adventure for any young wildlife enthusiast, a trip to these ecologically famous islands involves a considerable flight and then a lot of time (probably sleeping) on boats while you explore the different islands. The reward is sightings of an incredible variety of unique birds and animals, many of which lack natural predators and stay put when humans venture near. Go underwater and it's like snorkelling in your very own aquarium with sea horses, marine iguanas, hammerhead sharks and Galápagos penguins to name just a few of the creatures you will see.
Find coherent advice at www. lonelyplanet.com/ecuador/the-galapagos-islands. Supporting a Galápagos-focussed charity as you plan your trip may mean you are sent newsletters to inform and excite your kids.

3 Yellowstone National Park, USA

Whether it's bears or beavers, moose or mountain goats, elks or eagles, this park deserves its world-famous reputation for easy spotting of

wildlife living properly in the wild. Especially if you get off the beaten track or even camp. The park has excellent activities for children, including a Junior Ranger program (age-appropriate activities need to be completed for the Junior Ranger patch to be awarded – we want one!). It's also worth checking out the website for pre-trip fun and recommended reading.

The park's site has all the info you need: www.nps.gov/yell. Remember you are visiting wilderness and plan appropriately. Bring binoculars. Use the ranger stations to find out about the best locations for spotting.

4 *Queen Elizabeth National Park, Uganda*

Tree-climbing lions? Tick! Healthy numbers of hippos and elephants? Tick! Over 600 different bird species? You've got it... This is the place to come for guaranteed sightings of a huge range of African wildlife, a real-life geography lesson in the difference between savannah, wetlands and forests, and the chance to do all this without having to share it with too many of your fellow humans. You can also take a boat safari on the Kazinga Channel, giving your family a unique perspective on the many mammals, birds and reptiles coming to drink here.

The recommended place to stay is the Mweya Safari Lodge (www.mweyalodge.com); it has a pool – need we say more?

YOU DON'T HAVE TO BE A KID TO SUCCUMB TO THE CHARMS OF PANDAS AT PLAY IN CHENGDU

Top travel lists ●●● ●●●● ●●●●●●●●●

5 Refugio Nacional de Fauna Silvestre Ostional, Costa Rica

Hundreds, sometimes thousands, of olive ridley turtles come here to nest each year: keep the kids up late to watch this mass nesting and they will be wide-eyed for days. Your mini David Attenborough can also seek out urchins and anemones in the tidal pools, clock ghost crabs on the beach and indulge in a spot of birdwatching, all within easy reach of the hatching turtles. And then of course there's the rest of Costa Rica to explore with more turtles, one or two crocodiles, some amazing butterflies and plenty of opportunities for high adrenaline fun such as zip lining through forest canopies and white-water rafting. *Check out www.visitcostarica.com for good advice on planning your trip. The turtles nest between July and December.*

6 Goats in trees, Essaouira, Morocco

An extraordinary sight to behold, and bound to make the whole family chuckle, the prospect of goats in trees is a great excuse to explore Morocco as a whole. In short: the argan trees bear argan nuts; the goats like the nuts; the goats like the nuts so much they will climb to the top of the argan tree and balance there happily while they munch said nuts. Surely there should be a yoga move named after these nimble beasts. See them either on the Essaouira road or outside Taroudant.

Travel early in the morning to get the best 'views' and make sure your transport will accommodate a stop. Have change available to tip the farmers if you want a photo. More information on visiting Morocco can be found at www.visitmorocco.com.

YOU MIGHT CATCH A GLIMPSE OF A RUFOUS-TAILED HUMMINGBIRD IN COSTA RICA

7 Bat flights, Carlsbad Caverns, USA

Dusk falling, the sound of hundreds of thousands of wings flapping in unison as the air becomes dark and thick with a steady rising stream of bats, heading out to find the bugs they need to survive till the next day. Ever wondered what a 'bat tornado' feels like? Well, take your kids to Carlsbad Caverns in New Mexico and find out. Equally impressive is the bats' return flight, although that obviously requires an earlier start. On certain days of the year you can stay on after the bat flight and learn all about the night sky too. Mind-blowing, for kids big and small.

Find everything you need to know at www.nps.gov/cave. Teach your kids how sensitive the bats are and why it's important that all electronic devices are switched off.

8 Walkabout Wildlife Park, New South Wales, Australia

You can visit this park by day to see native Australian animals roaming free, but we recommend the Wild Night Out where you can camp in the park overnight. Not only does this give you better sightings of the animals (many of which are nocturnal), but the experience of toasting marshmallows on the campfire while friendly eyes watch you from the surrounding trees and then snuggling down in your cosy tent to the sound of possums, koalas and bilbies as they come out to play is something no child will ever forget.

If you do come during the day, the best chance of seeing animals is in the afternoon when they get fed; www.walkaboutpark.com.au has everything you need to plan your trip.

9 Monkey rescue, Pretoria, South Africa

What better way to bond with your own imps than helping with the care and conservation of over 100 species of primates in a monkey sanctuary? Volunteer as a whole family and you can can get involved with food preparation, enclosure cleaning and maintenance, behaviour observation and recording, and 'monkey time' while your furry friends play. Then tack on a trip to Kruger National Park to see animals in the wild as a well-earned reward for your hard work.

Suitable for families with children aged 13 and over; the family volunteer projects are run through PoD volunteer projects: www.podvolunteer.org.

What better way to bond with your own imps than helping with the care and conservation of over 100 species of primates in a monkey sanctuary?

10 Watching birds of prey, UK

Teach the kids the ancient art of falconry on a day out in the English countryside. As well as learning all about these magnificent birds of prey and how they survive in the wild, there are plenty of opportunities for your kids to get a sense of what falconry is all about through handling the hawks, owls and vultures, and experiencing the exhilarating thud of a bird landing on their fist. A must for fans of Harry Potter's Hedwig.

Suitable for kids seven and over; try www. thehawkingcentre.co.uk or www.birdonthehand. co.uk. ● By Imogen Hall

JONATHAN GREGSON © LONELY PLANET IMAGES

Top travel lists ● ● ● ● ● ● ● ● ● ● ● ● ● ● ● ●

151

Most accessible destinations

With the world's population rapidly ageing, businesses and tourism bodies are slowly realising it's not just the disabled who have access in mind when planning a trip.

1 Singapore

Singapore has to be the most accessible city in Asia and one of the most accessible cities in the world. Its universal code on barrier-free accessibility, in place for more than 20 years, plus increasing affluence have resulted in an infrastructure with stepless access to most buildings and no shortage of kerb cuts. Although power wheelchair-friendly taxis aren't common, the accessibility of the mass rail transit (MRT) and buses, for the visually as well as the motor impaired, makes them unnecessary. In Singapore, the question is not 'what is accessible?' but rather 'what isn't?' – from its street food hawker centres to its marvellous zoo.

The Disabled People's Association of Singapore has an excellent resources page on www.dpa.org.sg.

2 Barcelona, Spain

With the national tourism authority and Catalonia in particular pushing accessible travel, it's no surprise that wheelchair users have been flocking to Barcelona. With 80% of the metro stations and 100% of buses wheelchair-accessible, as well as a relatively flat and cobblestone-free old city, getting around is a breeze. What's more, wheelchair users not only jump to the front of the queue for attractions such as the breathtaking Sagrada Família, they often get in for free! You can roll the length of La Rambla and get around the famous Mercat de la Boqueria; even the beach has wheelchair access and people on hand to help.

Barcelona Turisme has a multilingual website dedicated to accessible travel, which has all the information you need to know: http://barcelona-access.cat.

3 Manchester, UK

Although it was the birthplace of the Industrial Revolution, much of central Manchester was rebuilt in the late 1990s, making smooth, wide, step-free pavements, as well as stepless entry into shops, restaurants and bars the norm – ideal for anyone with mobility requirements. Northern England's cultural hub is well served by accessible public transport, leaving you free to pay homage at Old Trafford, learn about our industrial roots at the Museum of Science and Industry or shop with the Goths at Affleck's. And if you've had enough of the city, the Peak District National Park, with well-developed facilities for disabled visitors, is less than an hour away. *Start planning at Visit England (www.visitengland.com/plan-your-visit/access-all), Open Britain (www.openbritain.net/northern-england) and DisabledGo (www.disabledgo.com). If you're heading to the great outdoors, check out www.peakdistrict.gov.uk/visiting/accessible-places-to-visit/access4all.*

4 Melbourne, Australia

With its highly accessible public transport system and compact city centre, Melbourne is one of the most accessible cities in the world. Visit the sporting capital of Australia armed with Lonely Planet's pilot accessibility guide, *Accessible Melbourne*, a free e-book that includes the most up-to-date advice for travellers with special needs. Discover Melbourne's best wheelchair-friendly restaurants, enjoy spectacular scenery along the Great Ocean Road, and visit one of the world's best zoos as well as many of the parks that progressive Parks Victoria is opening up to visitors with access issues.

Download our free e-book at www.lonelyplanet.com/accessible-melbourne and plan your outdoors adventures here: http://parkweb.vic.gov.au/accessibility.

THE SAGRADA FAMÍLIA IS JUST ONE OF BARCELONA'S MANY ACCESSIBLE ATTRACTIONS

Top travel lists ●●●● ●●● ●●●●●●●● ●●●

5 Galápagos & Amazonia, Ecuador

So you've been watching David Attenborough and thought you'd never be able to access such places in the flesh? Wrong! Lenín Moreno, paraplegic vice president of Ecuador (2006–13) and Nobel Peace Prize nominee did amazing work to improve the lives of disabled people throughout his country. Quito may not be as accessible as the average Western city, but largely thanks to Moreno inroads have been made. But if you want to explore Amazonia, the Andes and the Galápagos, go zip lining or even cross the border into Peru to visit Machu Picchu, you'll need to go on an organised tour. *South America for All (www. southamericaforall.com) has been operating tours for the mobility- and hearing-impaired for the last seven years, starting in Ecuador and now branching out into Peru.*

6 Playa del Carmen, Mexico

'Where?' you may ask. One hour from Cancún International Airport, Playa Del Carmen is a far cry from its brash neighbour, yet still has accessible hotels and an accessible beach furnished with beach wheelchairs. Even if you can't swim, there's adaptive equipment to allow you to go snorkelling to enjoy the coral reef and green turtles. With everything within walking distance, there's no need for accessible transport. But the main reason for coming here is to visit the nearby and largely wheelchair-accessible Mayan archaeological sites, Chichén Itzá and Tulum, a rare chance for the mobility-impaired to get up close to ancient ruins. *Accessible transport is limited, so go through respected tour operator Cancún Accesible (www. cancunaccesible.com), which provides airport transfers and tours to the sites, hires all manner of equipment, and offers well-informed advice.*

7 Sicily, Italy

Italy might not spring to mind as a very accessible destination nor as one associated with adventure travel. Home to a Tactile Museum and Europe's only sensorial botanic garden, as well as Europe's largest active volcano, Mt Etna, Sicily is breaking new ground, so to speak. But it doesn't stop there: the blind, visually and motor-impaired can enjoy scuba diving, 4WD off-road driving, traditional Sicilian fishing and olive oil making – not to mention the gastronomic delights normally associated with Italy. Indeed, two Guinness world records have been set here: first paraplegic to dive to 59m and first blind woman to dive to 41m! *Seable (www.seable.co.uk) is a well-established and respected tour operator with partners around the world and operates in association with Sicilian charity LIFE (Life Improvement for Everyone).*

8 San Diego, USA

With the Americans with Disabilities Act having just celebrated its 25th anniversary, much of the USA's infrastructure is accessible, but our pick is San Diego. Laid out along the classic grid system, generally flat and with a fully accessible

MARVEL AT THE TOWERING BAMBOO GROVES IN ECUADOR

9 Ljubljana, Slovenia

Slovenia's flat and largely pedestrianised capital, served by accessible electric vehicles, is well worth a visit. Its bus network is well endowed with audio and video stop announcements, complemented by Braille bus stop signs and a network of city centre tactile paths. The city's main drawcard, the 16th-century Ljubljana Castle – a tactile model of which can be found in the courtyard with descriptions in Braille – is reached via a funicular (free for the disabled and companion) or train, both wheelchair-accessible. Many of Jože Plečnik's famous bridges have recently been made accessible, and were joined in 2010 by the award-winning Butchers' Bridge, which allows wheelchair users access to boats.

The City of Ljubljana paired up with UK charity DisabledGo to produce an online access guide: www. disabledgo.com/organisations/ljubljana/main-2.

10 Vienna, Austria

Like many European cities, Vienna is steeped in history, being the centre of the former Habsburg Empire and the musical heart of Europe. Unlike many of its counterparts, however, its cobblestones have been removed, as have many of the kerbs. The refurbished city is both flat and compact, with most central shops and cafes fully accessible. Getting around is relatively easy with elevators to the metro and plenty of low-floor trams. Most museums and places of interest are fully accessible, including the must-see Schloss Schönbrunn.

Find all you'll need to know at www.wien.info/en/ travel-info/accessible-vienna.● By Martin Heng, Lonely Planet's Accessible Travel Manager

trolley (tram) system, it also boasts a balmy year-round 18–27°C climate. The historic Gaslamp Quarter is very wheelchair friendly, as is the massive Balboa Park (incorporating the slightly hilly San Diego Zoo), but it's the miles of beachfront promenade with beach wheelchairs available – including a motorised one with caterpillar tracks at Mission Beach! – that are the main attraction.

Check out http://access-sandiego. org and www.sandiego.org/plan-your-trip/travel-guides/accessible-traveling.aspx. To explore further up the coast, see www.wheelingcalscoast. org/county.php?county=1.

Top travel lists ●●●● ●●● ●●●●●●●●●

Super sleeper trains

Sadly, sleeper trains are on the decline, but there are still some awesome overnighters you can do by rail.

1 London, England–Fort William, Scotland

Close your eyes on a chaos of traffic-jammed, office-crammed streets; open them again on a morning of heather-daubed, deer-scampered mountain and moor... The Caledonian Sleeper, which runs from London to northern Scotland, isn't a train ride, it's an escape – an overnight teleport from hubbub to Highlands. After Edinburgh, the route splits into three strands, bound variously for Inverness, Aberdeen and Fort William; the latter is the most spectacular, wending via Loch Lomond and over Rannoch Moor – where the tracks float atop a sponge of roots and brushwood – to arrive at the foot of Ben Nevis, the UK's highest peak.
The Caledonian Sleeper leaves Euston station at around 9pm Sunday–Friday; there is no Saturday departure. See www.sleeper.scot.

2 Moscow, Russia–Beijing, China

The Trans-Siberian isn't the most classic sleeper, it's the most classic train fullstop. It's a leviathan locomotive, taking its time to cross the planet's least hospitable terrain, chugging via unpronounceable Russian cities, the world's deepest lake and chilling yet oddly captivating Siberian sprawl. There are three lines of the railway; the most interesting is the Trans-Mongolian route, which links Moscow to Beijing via Ulaanbaatar. That said, much of the point is experiencing life on the train itself, buying sausages from station vendors, learning card games from your carriage mates and chatting until dawn over hot tea – or a vodka or three.
The weekly Trans-Mongolian leaves Moscow every Tuesday night. The journey takes 6.5 days.

3 Rome–Syracuse, Italy

Few modes of transport rival the romance of the railway, except maybe boats. Fortunate, then, that this Italian overnighter combines both. The sleeper train from the Eternal City to Sicilian Syracuse (Siracusa) – via some cracking Calabrian coastline and gurgly Mt Etna – is physically hoisted onto a ferry in order to cross the Straits of Messina. The passage takes about 30 minutes: you can either catch some fresh Mediterranean air on deck or stay in your couchette, squirrelled away in the ferry's hold, riding a train on a boat for the most multi-layered of travel experiences.
The sleeper leaves Rome daily at around 9.30pm, arriving at Syracuse at around 9.35am. See www. trenitalia.com for more info.

4 New Delhi–Agra, India

If the thought of jostling with the hoi-polloi on

THE GHAN CHUGS THROUGH THE
VIVID AUSTRALIAN OUTBACK

a regular train makes you shudder, the Palace on Wheels is for you. Seven days of travelling like an Indian raja – luxurious quarters, 24-hour butler service – should spoil you for life. The experience takes you on a tour of ancient Rajasthan, a fabled realm of maharajas, majestic forts and lavish palaces. Starting in New Delhi and ending at the Taj Mahal in Agra, the journey includes such highlights as the jewellery capital of Jaipur, India's tiger country and the Lake Palace at Udaipur. It's a mammoth stretch, taking seven days from start to finish, so be prepared to make yourself comfortable and relish all that royal heritage in style.

The Palace on Wheels departs from Safdarjung station in Delhi every Wednesday, from September to April. Visit www.palaceonwheelsindia.com.

Top travel lists ● ● ● ● ● ○ ● ●
● ● ● ● ● ● ● ● ●

JOSH McCULLOCH © GETTY IMAGES

THE FAMOUS MORANT'S
CURVE NEAR LAKE LOUISE
IN BANFF NATIONAL PARK

5 Johannesburg–Cape Town, South Africa

The Blue Train is jolly nice indeed. This opulent tourist loco glides between Pretoria and Cape Town, showing off South Africa's spectacular scenery in style. But you pay for the wood-panelled privilege – about US$1400 to be precise. Which seems a bit unnecessary when the perfectly serviceable Shosholoza Meyl does virtually the same journey for less than a twentieth of the price. The cheaper trains run from Johannesburg, but otherwise follow an identical route. Granted, there are fewer butlers on board, but you're more likely to get chatting to the locals.

The Shosholoza Meyl journey is 1530km and takes 27 hours. Trains run Wednesdays, Fridays and Sundays. See www.shosholozameyl.co.za.

6 Toronto–Prince Rupert, Canada

This isn't a train ride, it's a history lesson. Canada was populated by rail; when immigrants arrived on the eastern seaboard, they travelled onwards on the pioneering tracks heading west. The Canadian is the big daddy – the five-day, thrice-weekly, country-spanning service from Toronto to Vancouver, crossing great plains, Rocky Mountains and a lot of splendid empty in between. To up the epic-ness, change onto the Skeena service at Jasper. This is Canada's most scenic ride, wending amid the high peaks and stopping at truly remote, fascinating townships en route.

The Skeena takes two days. See www.viarail.ca for information on both routes.

7 Nice, France–Moscow, Russia

Linking the Mediterranean to the Moskva River, this is Europe's longest train journey – 3315km and almost 50 hours of rattling across the continent. Look out the window: there's the sparkling French Riviera, the Italian exquisiteness of Milan and Verona, the snow-tickled Alps around Innsbruck, grand Vienna, the Czech-Polish border city of Bohumin, the Belarussian capital of Minsk and Smolensk, one of Russia's oldest cities. It's an educational unspooling of West-meets-East, showing where borders have softened, and where they have not (you'll need a visa just to pass through Belarus), and reminding you why it's far more fun to go by train.
Trains run once weekly: the westbound train from Moscow departs Thursdays; the eastbound from Nice on Saturdays. Tickets from www.russianrailways.com.

8 Darwin–Adelaide, Australia

You can fly to Australia's Red Centre. But a plane hop doesn't do justice to the endless unfolding of crimson and umber that reminds you where – and how small – you are. Reaching this big nation's belly by train allows a proper appreciation of its scale, and of the hardships endured by those who went before. The Ghan, which links northern Darwin to southern Adelaide, is named for the Afghan cameleers who hoiked goods to in-the-middle Alice Springs before the railway existed. For four days, watch the red rock and roos roll by, and be glad you're not covering the 2979km on foot.
The Ghan has three classes: deluxe Platinum sleepers, Gold sleepers and Red reclining daynighter seats. See www.greatsouthernrail.com.au.

9 Chicago–San Francisco, USA

Named after the ancient Greek god of the west wind, the California Zephyr blows westward too, carrying pioneer spirit (if no longer real pioneers) from Chicago to Emeryville, near San Francisco, via an array of heavenly views. On its 3924km journey, it negotiates snow-sprinkled mountains, raging white-water, vertiginous gorges, hostile desert and an engineering marvel of tunnels and switchbacks. It even masters the Continental Divide. This is the route that, in 1869, first linked the east and west of the USA.
The California Zephyr runs daily; the route takes 51.5 hours non-stop. See www.amtrak.com.

10 Hanoi–Ho Chi Minh City, Vietnam

Though this train runs on tracks built by French colonialists in the 1930s, its spirit is 100% Vietnamese. They call this top-to-toe line the Reunification Express, because when it resumed service in 1976 – after years of US bombardment – it rumbled across a freshly reunited nation. And what a rumble, a 1726km journey from the frenetic streets of northern Hanoi to sizzling southern Ho Chi Minh City, via the shores of the South China Sea, the formerly country-dividing DMZ, historic Hué, sandy Nha Trang and untold numbers of rice paddies, water buffaloes and bucolic scenes.
Hanoi–Ho Chi Minh City takes around 30 hours. Popular Hoi An is not on the railway; it's 30km by bus from Danang station. ● *By Sarah Baxter*

Best places to test your survival skills

Can't sit still while on holiday? Embark on one of these ten adventures and we reckon you'll be begging for a beach and a good book afterwards.

1 Bear Grylls Survival Academy, Zimbabwe

Bear Grylls is on his way to creating an entire army of survivalists who are overly enthusiastic about freezing their butts off and eating disgusting things. There are currently more than a dozen Bear Grylls Survival Academies around the globe, where instructors have been handpicked by Grylls and, in many cases, served as crew or technical advisors on his shows. Our favourite is an intense five-day course near Victoria Falls in Zimbabwe. Alongside nine others, you will be issued your Bear Grylls survival knife and taught everything from treating rancid water and building a shelter in the bush to lighting a fire — all while being watched by rhinos, lions and elephants. *You'll need to know how to swim and be able to carry a 20lb (9kg) pack for about an*

PADDLE TO VICTORY AT THE AMAZON RIVER ANNUAL INTERNATIONAL RAFT RACE IN PERU

© RODRIGO RODRICH

*hour over rough terrain. See www.
beargryllssurvival academy.com/
africa.*

2 Speight's Coast to Coast, New Zealand

We love an adventure race named
after a beer. But don't be fooled —
the Speight's Coast to Coast, which
happens every February, is a 243km
multi-sport adventure race on New
Zealand's rugged South Island that
takes two full days to complete. From
the start at Kumara Beach, you and
about a thousand others will run,
bike, and kayak across stunning
Lord of the Rings landscapes until
you end up at Brighton Beach near
Christchurch. But what we love most
about the iconic 33-year-old event is
that it's achievable for mortals — the
spirit among competitors is classic
Kiwi enthusiasm and the atmosphere
is more fun-run than Iron Man.
*You can compete alone, or in a team
of two or three. See www.coasttocoast.
co.nz.*

3 Fuego y Agua Hunter Gatherer Survival Run, Nicaragua

With a tag line 'adapt or die', this
80km race — sometimes held in the
USA, sometimes in Nicaragua — sees
competitors climb, swim, dig and run
over brutal wilderness terrain. This
is no co-worker team-building outing

so don't sign up unless you have some endurance
race experience. Unlike other hardcore adventure
races, it places a premium on intelligent problem-
solving, and the permitted-gear list looks more like
something you'd find on a survival course than an
ultramarathon.
*Race organisers suggest boning up on climbing
trees and making a bowdrill fire, and among
'required items' is a pencil. See www.fuegoyagua.
org.*

4 Amazon River Annual International Raft Race, Peru

This three-day event deep in the Peruvian jungle
is almost as fun to watch as it is to participate in.
Covering 180km, more than 40 teams of four build
their own raft out of local balsawood logs (locals
are on hand to help) and then paddle downstream,
stopping only to sleep along the way. But it's not
as simple as it sounds — only one foreign team
has won in 17 years. After a pre-race dinner and
a little dance party, it's off to bed to rest up for
the journey. Then you spend the next three days
learning more than you could ever want about your
raft mates, and trying to become the second team
ever to beat the locals.
*If you haven't organised a team in advance, you
can just show up in Nueva Esperanzo and look for
a team that needs paddlers. Contact the tourism
dept of Loreto, Peru for more information.*

5 Bob Cooper Outback Survival, Australia

Where better to test your survival skills than in
one of the world's most inhospitable places: the
Australian outback. And who better to teach you the
bush skills you need to survive 30+°C heat, deadly
snakes, and the sort of remoteness that makes men
go crazy, than Australia's most legendary survivalist,
Bob Cooper. Cooper gets deep here, touching not
only on how to avoid toxic flora and fauna, but

also the psychology of survival. Even Cooper's basic three-day Wilderness Survival course — a prerequisite for one of his more intense eight-day challenges — will test your skills in fire building, navigation, foraging and building shelters.

Cooper's advanced courses in the rugged Pilbara region allow participants to put all their skills to the test in a realistic survival scenario. See www.bobcoopersurvival.com.

6 Expedition Alaska, USA

Any kind of trip to Alaska is an adventure. But every June, the organisers of Expedition Alaska put on what many consider to be the most challenging adventure race in the world. This seven-day event on the Kenai Peninsula covers roughly 500km and includes monster stretches of trekking, ocean crossings, white-water kayaking, packrafting, mountain biking, canyoneering, coasteering, and abseiling. Needless to say, it's experts only. Expedition Alaska is the ultimate test of fitness, outdoor survival skills and wits, in one of the world's most unforgiving wildernesses.

Sign up early — they only take 100 competitors (in teams of two or more) and priority is given to those who have participated in Expedition Idaho. See www.expeditionak.com.

7 Docastaway Desert Island Experience, worldwide

Docastaway hand-picks an ever-changing list of islands and beaches around the world that allows you to experience desert island isolation, with as little or as much in the way of resources as you want. In fact, it offer two styles of trips, 'Comfort' and 'Adventure'. While both are aimed at those seeking total seclusion, the 'Adventure' trips are genuine survival experiences that take place on remote deserted islands in places with imaginary names, so as not to divulge their actual location. And if you choose the 'Extreme' option, there is a good chance you'll be making your own shelter. However, many islands have spartan bungalows or lean-tos and Docastaway will provide whatever other basics you need to look after yourself.

The menu of destinations changes all the time. Consult with Docastaway first on the sort of experience you are after and it will match you up with the perfect beach for your budget. See www.docastaway.com.

8 Tom Brown Jr's Tracker School, USA

Tom Brown Jr is a legend in the tracking and survival game, with a strong emphasis on the techniques and traditions of his Native American ancestors. His courses take place in the not-so-remote Pine Barrens of New Jersey but, after nearly 40 years in business, his services have been sought out by everyone from the police to potential contestants on the TV show *Survivor*. Brown teaches basic survival — building shelters, making fires, etc — as well as things like evasion and search and rescue. But it's his knack for tracking, a skill passed on to Brown by his own Apache grandfather, Stalking Wolf, that has earned him his reputation.

Brown's 'Standard' six-day survival course is a prerequisite for all other courses and includes lessons in track analysis, the ability to move silently through the forest, and how to follow a track. See www.trackerschool.com.

9 Clipper Round the World Yacht Race

This is the Vendée Globe for Everyman: complete novices are invited to simply sign up, take the intensive six-day training course covering everything from cooking to rigging, and then embark on as many or as few of the eight stages as you think you can handle – and afford. This 20-year-old race is a way for those who don't have the skill or cash to do such a thing independently to experience sailing's greatest test. You will join a crew on one of twelve identical 21m yachts, with an experienced skipper at the helm, and then rotate through every role on the boat. The reward is cutting through the open ocean at up to 35 knots, through the Doldrums, past Cape Horn, or through the Roaring Forties. *A spot on the yacht for the entire year-long, 40,000 nautical mile race is about £45,000 (US$66,690); individual legs, which last anywhere from 18 to 40 days, cost between £5000 (US$7400) and £6000 (US$8890). See http:/ clipperroundtheworld.com.*

Top travel lists ● ● ● ● ● ●
● ● ● ● ● ● ●

10 Polar Explorers' North Pole expedition

The only 'summit' that really rivals Everest in terms of bucket-list cred is the North Pole. Sure, all the climbing is measured in lines of latitude, but the cold, bleak journey has been capturing the imagination of explorers for far longer than any mountain. Illinois-based Rick Sweitzer was the first person ever to lead a guided dogsled-ski expedition for amateurs to the North Pole in 1993 and has since, through his company Polar Explorers, been putting together everything from five-day in-and-out ski tours to full 60-day expeditions. Sweitzer's crew is the best in the business, experts in cold-weather survival and suffering, but also known to host cocktail hours after a hard day on the ice. *Polar Expeditions' most popular expedition is the 'Last Degree' trip, a 14-day ski tour that covers the last 100km or so, and includes a helicopter ride back to civilisation. See www.polarexplorers.com.*

● *By Will Cockrell*

THE NORTH POLE IS THE ULTIMATE TERRAIN FOR FEATS OF ENDURANCE

MARTIN HARTLEY © GETTY IMAGES

The world's most extraordinary sleepovers

Sheer inventiveness and the sharing economy have opened up a new world of sublime and ridiculous places to spend the night.

1 Dog Bark Park Inn, Idaho, USA

When in Idaho, where you do feel like staying? In the stomach of an enormous beagle? You're in luck: we have just the place. Dog Bark Park Inn is the brainchild of two artistic dog lovers, and is an enormous structure – rather like a Trojan horse, but a dog, if you see what we mean. Things inside are dog-themed too, with dog-decorated cushions and dog-shaped biscuits. The owners specialise in 'chainsaw art', which isn't as terrifying as it sounds – they produce wooden sculptures of various breeds, available in the shop on site. 'Responsible pets, with well-behaved owners' are permitted.

Dog Bark Park is bookable via Airbnb or the owners' website (dogbarkparkinn.com), and costs US$98 per night for two people.

2 Dino Snores at the Natural History Museum, London, UK

London's Natural History Museum offers the chance to stay the night with the museum's famous bony dinosaurs. The children's sleepover includes a torch-lit trail of the Dinosaurs gallery and a live science show, while the grown-up version includes a three-course dinner, science shows, live music, bars,

SNOOZE AMONGST THE DINOSAURS AT LONDON'S NATURAL HISTORY MUSEUM

edible insect-tasting, and all-night monster movie marathon. The next morning there's breakfast and more entertainment. You can bed down anywhere in Hintze Hall: for the biggest thrill, snuggle up under the shadow of the blue whale skeleton.

Dino Snores events are for kids aged 7–11. Sleepovers cost UK£60 (children)/£180 (adults) and take place regularly; book ahead on nhm.ac.uk.

3 Nanuku Levu, Fiji

For the ultimate in tranquillity and romance, why not hire your own private 10-acre Fijian island, Nanuku Levu? With its ancient coconut palms and blindingly white sand, it's a daydream come to life. You won't be bothered by the neighbours: there are 15 miles of translucent, pale blue South Pacific between you and the nearest civilisation. The island has one small wooden beach hut, and a beachhouse, and your only visitors are likely to be turtles and huge seabirds. Boat transfer is included in the price.

This Fijian island costs £333 per night, bookable via Airbnb.com, which has various other private island rentals available.

4 A House for Essex, UK

Opened in 2015, the gold-roofed A House for Essex looks as though a piece of Russian architecture from the Red Square crossed with a gingerbread house has been transplanted to the north Essex coast. The house has been co-designed by Essex-raised artist Grayson Perry and the architectural practice FAT, to evoke a wayside chapel or folly. Perry has decorated the interior as if it belonged to an everywoman he's called Julie. Staying here is to be immersed in an imaginary life, and become a part of a work of art. It's more profound than your average holiday let.

A House for Essex is part of the Living Architecture project (living-architecture.co.uk/the-houses/a-house-for-essex/overview/, which has various other superbly out-there places to stay.

Top travel lists ● ● ● ● ● ● ● ● ● ● ● ● ● ● ● ● ○

IGLU-DORF IN ZERMATT
PROMISES A COOL BUT
COSY RECEPTION

5 Propeller Island, Berlin, Germany

Where else but Berlin would offer you some of the world's most mind-boggling beds? Propeller Island is the pseudonym used by German audio-visual artist Lars Stroschen, and one of his most popular projects is the Propeller Island City Lodge. Choose to sleep in a coffin, in the 'upside-down' room that messes with your perception, or have a snooze in a suspended bed. Plump for a room with electric wallpaper, a padded cell, or crank down an illuminated barrier to split a double bed into two. These choices are just the start, so take your pick for one of the weirder nights of your life. *Rooms at Propeller Island City Lodge (www. propeller-island.de) cost from €79-190 for a double.*

6 Roar & Snore at Taronga Zoo, Sydney, Australia

There are lots of choices of zoo sleepovers around the world, including nights in the bughouse at London Zoo and the chance to snuggle (well, almost) with snow leopards at the Bronx Zoo Family Overnight Safari (NYC). However, the pick of the bunch has to be Sydney's Roar & Snore. Here you nod off in luxury tented camps, complete with beds and wooden floors, with an astounding view of Sydney Opera House, the city and the Sydney

Harbour Bridge. Overnighters enjoy a gourmet buffet dinner, then a one-and-a-half-hour night safari, an extraordinary opportunity to explore the zoo without the crowds. *Roar & Snore (taronga.org.au/ taronga-zoo) costs A$320/205 for adults/children aged 5–17.*

7 Elqui Domos, Elqui Valley, Chile

All is well in a world where you have a wide choice of geodesic domes in which to spend the night. One of the most spectacular options is the Elqui Domos in Chile's Elqui Valley, famous for its star-spangled skies. There are seven geodesic canvas domes, each with removable roofs so that you can stargaze from beneath the duvet. If you can't make it to Chile, there are versions of these futuristic tents from Spain to South Wales.
Elqui Domos (elquidomos.cl) charges around US$155-190 for a double per night, and there are more geodesic options with Airbnb.

8 Boot Bed & Breakfast, Tasman, New Zealand

Has a boot-shaped hotel not been on your to-do list? Amend that and step into a living fairy tale in the epically beautiful area of Tasman in New Zealand. Looking like something out of a children's book, the boot sleeps two, with a cosy Hobbit-meets-Beatrix Potter-meets-twee feel. There's a sofa and open fire downstairs, where you can kick back in the toe area. Is this the ultimate boot-ique hotel?
The Boot is in the grounds of Jester House (jesterhouse.co.nz), and costs NZ$300 for two. It may also be booked through Airbnb.

9 Iglu-Dorf, Zermatt, Switzerland

Building starts on Iglu-Dorf ('igloo village') every November. It's made up of real snow igloos, near the smart Swiss resort of Zermatt, with incredible views over the Matterhorn. At 2700m, it offers various styles of igloo, including 'romantic' and 'family', but all are reliably chilly, though bedding is super-warm, on sheepskin and in sleeping bags. Decoration includes snow pictures carved into the walls, and flowers encased in ice. Jump in the Jacuzzi, with Matterhorn views, to warm up. And if you get tired of chilling out, you can join an igloo-building workshop.
Iglu-Dorf (iglu-dorf.com) opens from Christmas to April, and igloos cost from CHF109-479 per adult.

10 Underwater room at the Manta Resort, Zanzibar, Tanzania

Sleep with the fishes in the best possible sense. If you think sleeping underwater is impossible, think again. Various hotels worldwide are offering submarine experiences, but most spectacular is the Manta Resort in Zanzibar. A wooden hut stands alone in the ocean, 250m from a white-sand beach. It's on three levels, with a lounge upstairs, a rooftop for diving off, and a bedroom beneath sea level, with 360° views of pale blue sea and colourful tropical passersby such as bat fish and trumpet fish. We're just wondering what the sealife looking in makes of it all.
The underwater room at the Manta Resort (themantaresort.com) costs US$1500 per night for a double. ● By Abigail Blasi

Top travel lists ● ● ● ● ● ● ● ● ● ● ● ● ● ● ●

A journey into genius

Want to enter the world of a genius? Then take a trip with us to the places that put the greatest minds on the map.

1 Mozart's birthplace, Salzburg, Austria

Wolfgang Amadeus Mozart, the ultimate wunderkind, is synonymous with Salzburg. The childhood genius – who would later compose a host of classical masterpieces such as *The Marriage of Figaro*, *The Magic Flute* and *Requiem* – was born at Hagenauer House (also known as Geburtshaus) on 27 January 1756.

The house, where he lived with his sister and parents until the age of 17, has long been a popular museum. Set on three floors, it exhibits a collection of Mozart's letters, family portraits and an array of historical musical instruments, including his childhood violin.

The Salzburg Card gives visitors free museum entry, transport and discounted theatre tickets; for details see www.salzburg.info.

2 Freud's house, London, UK

OK, Sigmund Freud was Austrian and there is a sizeable museum in Vienna, but to really get into the mind of the founder of psychoanalysis, you need to go to London. Located on a quiet street in Hampstead, the Freud Museum looks like a rather ordinary Victorian house from outside, yet inside you'll find Freud's extensive collection of Egyptian ornaments, shelves filled with books and his original psychoanalyst couch. Amazingly, Freud only lived in the house for one year – he fled to London in 1938 after the Nazi annexation of Austria and died in 1939 – but his artefacts were preserved

by his daughter Anna Freud who lived in the house for 44 years.

The Freud Museum is open 12–5pm Wednesday to Sunday; learn more at www.freud.org.uk.

3 Einstein's apartment, Bern, Switzerland

German-born physicist, philosopher of science and all-round icon for crazy-haired geniuses everywhere, Albert Einstein lived in Bern from 1902 to 1909, which he called the happiest and most productive years of his life. Indeed, 1905 was his *annus mirabilis*, when he wrote four articles that changed modern physics and our views on space, time, and matter, including the special theory of relativity and his famous $E=mc^2$ equation. These earth-shattering papers were created in a modest apartment on Kramgasse, which is now the newly renovated Einstein House, home to his typewriter, telephone and some very well-worn passports.

Also in Bern, the Einstein Museum includes sections on his theories, relationships, the Holocaust and the atom bomb; for details see www.bhm.ch/en/exhibitions/einstein-museum.

4 Gandhi's ashram, Gujarat, India

'Generations to come', Einstein said, 'will scarce believe that such a man as this one ever in flesh and blood walked upon this Earth.' Not a scientific genius, Mohandas K Gandhi, known as 'Mahatma' or 'great soul', experimented with truth. No other place tells the tale of the little man who defeated the British Empire with his philosophy of *satyagraha* (nonviolent civil resistance) better than the Sabarmati Ashram. Gandhi lived here from 1917 to 1930. The ashram houses the 'My Life is My Message' photo gallery, Gandi's iconic *charkha* spinning wheel and 34,111 letters.

Sabarmati Ashram is 5km from Ahmedabad, where travellers can get an auto rickshaw or bus.

Top travel lists

THE AUSTRIAN TOWN OF SALZBURG, WHERE WOLFGANG MOZART WAS BORN

5 Kahlo's house, Mexico City, Mexico

A place of pilgrimage for art lovers, Casa Azul (Blue House) is where Frida Kahlo was born, lived and died. The house, built by her father in 1904, is located in the Coyoacán neighbourhood. Today, people flock to see her paintings, clothes, jewellery, household objects and the pre-Columbian art collected by her husband Diego Rivera. Best-known for her surreal self-portraits, Kahlo has become a 20th-century heroine, representative of Mexican, indigenous and feminist art. As she stated, 'I was born a bitch. I was born a painter.'
Casa Azul is at 247 Londres St; take the metro to Coyoacán.

6 Marx's pub, Brussels, Belgium

Although he was born in Germany and died in England, it was in Belgium that Karl Marx, along with his comrade Friedrich Engels, penned *The Communist Manifesto*. Legend has it that Marx, who lived in Brussels from 1845 to 1847, wrote the manifesto in the smoky backroom of le Cyne (the Swan), a public house where he educated workers. Aside from the swan statue that still graces the doorway, Marx wouldn't recognise the opulent Brasserie de l'Ommegang that now occupies 9 Grand Place. *Marx used Brussels*

because of its central location and modern railway; today Brussels to London St Pancras takes just two hours, see www.eurostar.com.

7 Curie's birthplace, Warsaw, Poland

Marie Curie, one of the greatest fighters against cancer, whose research continues to treat millions of patients worldwide, was a proud daughter of Warsaw. The first woman to win a Nobel Prize (1903) and be entombed in the Panthéon in Paris (1995), her heart was always in Poland. Famous for her pioneering research on radioactivity, the facade of her birthplace on Freta St has a mural depicting a baby holding a test tube with the two elements she discovered – polonium (named after Poland) and radium. This street is also home to the Maria Sklodowska-Curie Museum, which tells the tale of her life through exhibits and films in Polish, English and French.
Take a tour to discover another genius from Warsaw, Chopin: see www.warsawtour.pl.

8 Da Vinci's villa, Tuscany, Italy

Forget the *Mona Lisa* in Paris or *The Last Supper* in Milan, to see the real Leonardo da Vinci you need to go to the tiny village of Anchiano in Tuscany. It was here, among the vineyards and rolling hills, that the genius painter, architect and inventor drew his inspiration. The old country villa where Leonardo was born on 15 April 1452 has been recently renovated and transformed into an interactive museum. Down the road in Vinci is the Church of Santa Croce where Leonardo was baptised and the bigger Museo Leonardiano.
The reasonably-priced Hotel Monna Lisa is just 500m from the Museum Leonardiano and accessible from Florence, Sienna and Pisa.

THE SWIMMING POOL AT SALVADOR DALÍ HOUSE-MUSEUM IN PORT LLIGAT, CADAQUÉS

9 *Shakespeare's Globe, London, UK*

What could be more English than standing with a beer in hand, watching a Shakespeare play by the River Thames? Only tea with the Queen. Yes, 2016 marks 400 years since the death of William Shakespeare and this theatre on London's South Bank will be celebrating with a host of special performances and exhibitions. A reconstruction of the original Elizabethan playhouse from 1599, Shakespeare's Globe is an initiative by actor and director Sam Wanamaker and opened in 1997. It is now the undisputed home of Shakespeare in performance and also offers educational tours, a playground and a souvenir shop where you can buy a Hamlet hoodie. Word up!

Also on the South Bank, the Tate Modern plans to open its new 'pyramid' extension by the end of 2016s. See www.tate.org.uk.

10 *Dalí's house, Port Lligat, Spain*

Salvador Dalí said, 'There is only one difference between a madman and me. I'm not mad.' Indeed, there is a fine line between insanity and genius, which is made evident by Dalí's bizarre house, Casa Museu Dalí, in Port Lligat. Located just outside Girona near the French border, the house began in 1930 as a simple fishing hut, but over the decades Dalí added more rooms 'like a real biological structure'. The Spanish painter, famous for surrealist masterpieces, lived here until his wife Gala died in 1982. Packed with crazy objects (including a life-sized polar bear) and narrow corridors, it also has a tranquil courtyard, swimming pool and two egg-shaped towers.

The best way to get to Port Lligat is flying to Girona-Costa Brava airport, and then taking a local bus or taxi. ● *by Dan Savery Raz*

Top travel lists ● ● ● ● ● ● ●
● ● ● ● ● ● ● ●

Lonely Planet's favourite final frontiers

Fifty years ago, the Starship Enterprise boldly set out to discover new frontiers. In tribute, here's our pick of the world's next travel frontiers – these ones strictly for armchair travellers only...

1 Darién Gap, between Colombia & Panama

There's something disheartening about the fact that you can reach most of Latin America on one road; lucky then that the Pan-American Highway never managed to penetrate the jungles separating Panama and Colombia. There are two ways to bridge the void: the hard way, hiking and hopping along the rainforest-cloaked eastern coast by leaky boat, or the so-risky-as-to-be-insane-way, dodging narcotraffickers, guerrillas and anti-drugs agents in the dense jungles of the interior. For our money, the hard, coastal way should be challenging and rewarding enough. *Puerto Obaldia is the last outpost on the Panamanian side; launches run directly to Capurganá in Colombia, but you can hike several sections via La Miel and Sapzurro.*

DAHAB CANYON IN THE RED SEA

2 Boma National Park, South Sudan

Despite being one of the most dangerous countries in the world, South Sudan offers something that will make you the envy of travellers around the globe – a visa stamp so far enjoyed by just a handful of human beings. Tourist destinations in the world's newest country are still described as 'potential tourist destinations', an indication of how far off the map you have travelled. When the country is more settled, perhaps you'll be the one who makes the rumoured tourist sights – dramatic mountains, astonishing tribal encounters, amazing natural parks with teeming wildlife, and one of Africa's great wildlife migrations – into a reality.

Juba is the gateway to South Sudan, with a handful of flights from Dubai, Cairo and Nairobi.

3 Bikini Atoll, Marshall Islands

With photos of mushroom clouds billowing over the palms etched into the popular psyche, Bikini Atoll probably isn't the first tropical island paradise that leaps to mind. But over 60 years after the nuclear tests that put Bikini on the map, travellers are once again washing up on its shores. Well, close to its shores to be precise; the islands are only open to visitors on liveaboard dive safaris, visiting some of the most untouched reefs in the Pacific and the wrecks of the fleet of empty warships blown up in the Bikini tests.

Dive trips to Bikini Atoll run from April to November, departing from tiny Kwajalein Atoll in the western chain of the Marshall Islands.

4 Yali & Korowai Country, West Papua, Indonesia

In the impenetrable rainforests of West Papua, formerly Irian Jaya, there are said to be people who have never encountered anyone from the outside world. Boats and planes will ferry you as far as the coast of this jungle wilderness, but with the almost total absence of roads, from there on you are on your own. There's plenty of paperwork and money required to charter river boats and planes to reach the remote country inhabited by the Yali and Korowai people, but here you can get a taste of what life was like for the first explorers, when maps were to be drawn not followed.

As well as tribal encounters, you can seek never-seen-before creatures in Lorentz National Park, the largest reserve in the Asia-Pacific region.

5 Rub' al-Khali, Saudi Arabia

Nothing compares to the true emptiness of Saudi Arabia's Empty Quarter. The Rub' al-Khali is actually only the second-largest sand desert in the world, but this rolling sea of sand makes other deserts look like rush hour on the metro. Crossing requires a minimum of 40 days, even by camel, and with the difficulty of getting a visa for Saudi Arabia, most of the few dozen travellers who have attempted it since 1950 have opted for the side route from Oman to the United Arab Emirates.

Somewhere, lost in the Empty Quarter, are said to be the remains of Iram, the mystical city of pillars mentioned in the Quran.

Top travel lists ● ● ● ● ● ● ● ● ● ● ● ● ● ● ● ● ●

6 Nepal's newest climbing peaks

As a gesture of respect for local beliefs, the summit of Machhapuchhre is never claimed by mountaineers, but in 2014 Nepal opened up 104 new climbing peaks for the very first time. Predictably, the mountains named for Edmund Hillary (7681m) and Tenzing Norgay (7916m) grabbed most of the attention, leaving 102 peaks for people looking for their very own first ascent. Unlike on Everest, there are no ice doctors here to lay out fixed ropes and ladders across chasms, but lower climbing fees put these Himalayan monsters within reach of ordinary climbers who come for the love of rock, ice and adventure.

The Nepal Mountaineering Association (www. nepalmountaineering.org) oversees the climbing of all peaks in Nepal; see the website for all the fees, rules and regs.

7 Dahab, Egypt

What's this? A well-known tourist hotspot on a list of final frontiers? Well, in this case, the final frontier is way, way down in the abyss. The intercontinental trench that plunges off the coast of Dahab has become *the* place to set a scuba

GET AWAY FROM ABSOLUTELY EVERYTHING IN SAUDI ARABIA'S RUB'AL-KHALI

diving record, with the current medal held by Egyptian Ahmed Gabr, who reached a staggering 332.35m in September 2014. What you encounter down there is anyone's guess, but you can't encounter it for long. The journey down takes a quarter of an hour; returning to the surface takes nearly 15 hours. Bring a (waterproof) book is our advice...

Despite a tense security situation, the reefs off Dahab remain one of the world's top diving destinations, home to the famous – and famously dangerous – Blue Hole.

8 North Hamgyong Province, North Korea

As the world's most infamous state, and official nemesis of *Team America*, the Democratic People's Republic of Korea might seem an unlikely holiday destination, but a trickle of travellers still brave unbelievable amounts of red tape to visit one of the last true Communist regimes. Trips to the capital, Pyongyang, are almost mainstream, despite an army of resident minders who ensure you only see 'approved' sights. More exciting are trips into North Korea's unseen northeast, where you can be one of the handful of tourists to experience the sights of Chongjin, the secretive 'City of Iron', and the eerily empty beach resorts around Mt Chilbo.

Chongjin is only open to tours for a few days a year, with travellers coming by rickety charter plane (eek!) from Pyongyang, or by road from China, via Rason.

9 Chernobyl, Ukraine

Chernobyl wasn't always a travel frontier; it took the catastrophic events of 26 April 1986 to drive every human being from the 2600 sq km Chernobyl Nuclear Power Plant Zone of Alienation. As radiation levels have dropped, groups have started exploring the abandoned cities around the Chernobyl nuclear plant – and with a name like 'Zone of Alienation', how could you resist? Today, you can get within 200m of the concrete sarcophagus encasing Reactor 4 – but no closer because of residual radiation – and wander (carefully) through apocalyptic abandoned cities, now taken over by deer, wolves, boar and wild horses.

Trips to the exclusion zone leave from Kyiv; for overnight stays, consider a stop at the austere InterInform Hotel Agency in Chernobyl. Check travel advisories due to the political situation in Ukraine.

10 Space, the final... well you know the rest

Fifty years after the first episode of *Star Trek* and space remains the final frontier... but it's getting closer. Despite the tragic crash of Virgin Galactic's *VSS Enterprise*, dozens of companies are spending millions to turn space tourism to a reality. Space Adventures is the first company to successfully transport its clients outside earth's atmosphere, with seven civilian astronauts since 2001, but others are close behind. The only drawback is the price tag – an estimated US$20–40 million per passenger, though Virgin Galactic hopes to undercut the market with fares of just US$250,000.

If you have a spare US$20 million or so lying around, contact Space Adventures (www. spaceadventures.com); their latest offerings include a circuit around the moon. ● By Joe Bindloss

Top travel lists ● ● ● ● ● ● ● ● ● ● ● ● ● ● ●

Best luxe experiences for budget travellers

Don't hit the brakes on your expensive tastes. Salvation lies in these affordable luxuries: star-spangled dining, castle sleeps and VIP treatment, all tailored for limited travel budgets.

POTPOURRI PETALS IN FRAGRANT GRASSE

1 Thermal bath for less in Reykjavík, Iceland

Melting into a naturally heated pool is a classic Icelandic experience. Best known is the Blue Lagoon near Reykjavík, but you can soothe your muscles without shedding all those kronur. Head to Nauthólsvík instead: this dainty strip of white sand has a pool of simmering seawater and a couple of hot tubs. The admission charge elicits as ardent a sigh of delight as the silky water: it's free in summer and in winter is just Ikr500; compare that to Ikr5400 for the most basic package at the Blue Lagoon. *Temperatures in Iceland rarely strike 20°C, even in summer, so bring layers on your Reykjavik bathing excursion. Size up the hot springs on www.nautholsvik.is.*

2 Budget-friendly fragrance in France

Quality perfume doesn't come cheap, and bespoke blended scents bust the bank balance even more – unless you follow your nose to the French Riviera. Centuries ago, abundant blooms and Mediterranean sunshine made the town of Grasse a centre for perfume-making. These days, travellers hoping to cloak themselves in fine fragrance still linger among Grasse's cobbled alleys and apricot-coloured buildings. Buying perfume from the source means rock-bottom prices, and workshops allow you to blend your very own scent. *It's €45 for a perfume workshop and 100ml of*

is the real deal: a 12th-century fortification that has seen sieges, explosions and ownership scuffles aplenty. Burg Stahleck has been raising its portcullis for visitors for decades, in between stints as a military hospital. Best of all, you can enjoy this family-friendly youth hostel accommodation and its superlative views without having to stand and deliver your purse.

Dorm beds cost €21.50 at this river-view château; book well ahead on www.jugendherberge.de/en/ youth-hostels/bacharach390/shortportraet.

4 Michelin stars for spare change in Hong Kong, China

If your belly rumbles only for globally acclaimed cuisine, follow the fragrant steam towards Hong Kong's Tim Ho Wan. Dim sum lovers swear by the barbecue pork buns and golden-fried turnip cakes of the world's cheapest Michelin-starred restaurant. Now a global sensation, chef and founder Mak Kwai Pui has new branches in Singapore, Sydney and Melbourne. Go now while the original is still the best.

Be sure to arrive early to secure your place in a ticketed queuing system.

5 Personalised cocktails in London, UK

Your thirst is fickle, your palate easily bored. Instead of paying hand-over-fist for the same old gin fizz, how about a devoted mixologist catering to your every whim? In a bare-brick cellar in the British capital, your capricious tastebuds are BYOC's command. Pay the entry fee and bring a bottle of booze that's gathering dust. Expert mixologists will draw on their alchemist's chest of syrups, salts and cordials to craft cocktails according to your mood.

The entry fee for BYOC is £25 – it beats a personal cocktail chef and at London drinks prices, you'll easily sip your money back. Learn more on www.byoc.co.uk.

your own personal fragrance at Galimard's Studio des Fragrances (www.galimard.com/index.php/en/ creez-votre-parfum/a-grasse). That's better than half the price of a bottle of Chanel No 5.

3 Cheap sleeps in a castle in Germany

You don't need celebrity clout to commandeer a castle in the Rhine Valley. Fabulous fortifications abound in this rugged green slice of western Germany, and even travellers with light wallets can bed down in Burg Stahleck. This spiky-turreted castle

6 VIP for free in Las Vegas, USA

Cover charges, resort fees, a little flutter turned all-night bender... Sin City sinks serious dollars. But you can sashay into nightclubs even after you've lost your shirt – just sign up for Free Vegas Club Passes. They'll put you down for free and VIP entry and tip you off about the night's locations by SMS. Ladies and gents can enjoy free entry to some usually wallet-wilting nightspots, and the ladies might get a few free drinks too. As if you needed more of an excuse to misbehave.

Once your name's on the list, it's all about looking the part: don your flashiest shoes and sign up at www.freevegasclubpasses.com.

7 Budget spa bliss in Fez, Morocco

Buffing, exfoliating and massaging until your muscles turn to butter – nowhere does it better than Morocco. Riads and hotels are keen to cash in on travellers hungry for a hammam experience, but if you follow the locals you can spend perhaps 20 dirhams (instead of hundreds). Arm yourself with a towel, soap and small change to tip attendants and rent a *kiis* (a scrub glove that will polish you like marble). Once you're through the doors, alternate between warm, hot and cool rooms and rinse

LIVE IT LARGE IN VEGAS – WITHOUT SPENDING THE BIG BUCKS

lavishly. Throw in a few dirhams for gommage with olive oil soap and you've got a royal scrubdown at pauper prices.

Get sudsy in traveller-friendly Ain Azleten Hammam (Talaa Kebira, Ain Azleten, Fez; entry Dh40).

8 Low-season safari in East Africa

Travel in low season. You've heard this wheeze before: lower prices, but severe penalties when it comes to weather and sights, right? Not so in East Africa, where venturing out on safari in rainy season offers more than shaving off money and crowds. The wet seasons (March to June and October to December) also have luminous sunsets and plenty of animals nurturing their young – excellent reasons to brave the rain (which, by the way, is patchy rather than perpetual downfall). You don't need to camp, self-drive or give up on luxe aspects like guided game drives, but you can save up to 40%.

Pack your raincoat and head on over to www.go2africa.com to scout rainy season deals. If you're flexible, last-minute deals score even more money off.

9 A sauna of your own in Sweden

In Scandinavia, saunas aren't luxury,

Once your name's on the list, it's all about looking the part: don your flashiest shoes

they're a way of life. These muscle-soothing hot rooms are considered so intrinsic to good health that they are built into hotels and apartments. And even in notoriously expensive Sweden you can snap up not only mid-range accommodation with sauna facilities, but your own private sauna. Apartments with private saunas in the lakeside winter sports haven Åre start at Skr4045 (US$490) for a week, beating the price of Swedish spa hotels.

If pillowy snowdrifts and sauna sessions are a match made in heaven, plan your Sweden trip for mid-March. Refine your accommodation search to find a private sauna on skistar.com.

10 Rock-bottom ryokan in Japan

The words 'shoestring ryokan' suggest hard tatami sleeping mats with little of Japan's famed *omotenashi* (hospitality). But a traditional inn experience can be enjoyed for a fraction of the usual price, without forfeiting hot baths and sublime in-room dining. Start by tweaking the location: ryokan-seekers are drawn to Kyoto, city of swaying lanterns and cherry-lipped geisha. Some plum deals for luxury ryokan lie further afield, like Sera Bekkan in Hiroshima. A night in a traditional room, with a feast served right to your bedroom plus bathing facilities to simmer in, costs a mere ¥10,000 (US$85).

Book well in advance for a trip during spring's cherry blossom season or Japan's autumn colours (mid-September to early November). Find a ryokan on www.japaneseguesthouses. com. By Anita Isalska

Top travel lists

Most iconic 20th-century houses

When is a museum not a museum? These modern masterpieces are all the more intriguing for once being loved and lived-in homes.

1 Villa Savoye, France

Fifty years after Le Corbusier's death, this home, built 1929–31, remains one of France's most significant 20th-century buildings. The architect's mantra was 'the house is a machine for living' and in this rigorous, severe work, the key tenets of the International Style, his 'five points', were writ large and loud. Design elements such as fluid indoor/outdoor spaces, a flat roof, simple lines and panoramic horizontal ribbon windows that visually harness the surrounding landscape were seen in a domestic context for the first time; the house still seems avant-garde today.

The house is in Poissy, around 40 minutes from Paris by car. It can also be reached by RER and bus. Plan your trip at www.villa-savoye.monuments-nationaux.fr.

2 Case Study House No 8: The Eames House, USA

Charles and Ray Eames' 1949 home and studio is both quintessentially Californian – understated, set in a meadow and surrounded by eucalypts, open to the sun and sea breezes – and symbolic of their

A LESSON IN GEOMETRY AT VILLA SAVOYE IN POISSY, FRANCE

BEST IN TRAVEL 2016

mid-century mission to democratise design. Clever construction methods maximised volume with minimal, mostly prefabricated materials. Rooms are, presciently, designed for multiple uses. Part bohemian home, part laboratory for their experiments in aesthetics and functionality, it's inspiring structurally but also a treat for the glimpses of the Eames' everyday life.

Visits are usually limited to the exteriors, though pre-arranged personal tours, US$275 for two, give you full access to the interiors and their collections.

3 The Aalto House, Finland

This house in the Helsinki seaside suburb of Munkkiniemi was the family home of Finland's beloved design duo, Alvar and Aino Aalto, from 1936. It's simple, uncluttered, but enticingly warm, and served as a prototype for much of Alvar Aalto's future work, combining functionalism with the architect's rapidly emerging humanism and environmental consciousness. The couple's experimental thinking and deep practicality are revealed in a walk-in wardrobe, a quirky double-sided china cabinet and innovations in insulation and orientation. Unlike many other early Modernist masterpieces, there is a strong sense of the local, with many decorative elements recalling and celebrating Finnish craft traditions.

Studio Aalto, the architect's 1955 studio, is a short walk away and combined tickets are available; guided tours run twice a day in summer, see www.alvaraalto.fi.

4 Villa Tugendhat, Czech Republic

Mies van der Rohe's 1930 villa in the Brno suburbs is a paean to space and light, doing away with supporting walls entirely, care of the architect's ground-breaking iron framework. Not only is the structure revolutionary, but so is its jettisoning of traditional interior decoration. Instead, luxurious, naturally beautiful materials form many of the functional surfaces, like the translucent, light-responsive African onyx wall in the living area. Furnishings, designed specially for the house in collaboration with Lilly Reich, combine tubular steel with rare woods and jewel-coloured leather; their characteristic 'Brno' chair is still in production today.

Book online in advance at www.tugendhat.eu for a coveted place on a guided tour; if you miss out, the exteriors are reason enough to visit in themselves.

5 Villa Necchi Campiglio, Italy

This 1930s villa, the masterwork of eccentric Rationalist Piero Portaluppi, dramatically cloistered by towering magnolias and high walls, makes for a seductive glimpse into the dark glamour of Milan's pre-war years. Its theatrical interiors mix unusual, ambitiously forward-thinking ideas – a terrarium-lined sun room must have set those Milanese tongues wagging – with haunting quotidian details. Closets are stuffed with pretty frocks and fur coats and steamer luggage is ever at the ready. A collection of equally evocative 20th-century artworks, Morandi and Di Chirico among them, grace the walls.

Open from Wednesday to Sunday, 10am to 6pm, with guided tours on demand; be sure to leave time to relax in the lush, fragrant garden.

Top travel lists ● ● ● ● ● ● ● ●
● ● ● ● ● ● ● ● ●

6 Dar Sebastian, Tunisia

Back in the day, Frank Lloyd Wright and Elsa Schiaparelli heaped praise on this beachside Modernist-Orientalist fantasia, dreamt up by Romanian millionaire George Sebastian from 1920 to 1932. Its airy, sexy spaces welcomed artists, celebrities, world leaders and fashion shoots throughout the 20th century. Little original furniture remains, and its luxurious interiors are careworn, but the central colonnaded swimming pool, its groin-vaulted ceilings and the 'party bathroom' – mirrors and a baptistery-like four-seater bath – are still a knockout.

Wandering the villa and grounds, now Hammamet's International Culture Centre, 3km from Hammamet town centre, is a delight – just don't expect anything in the way of meaningful signage or curation.

7 The Glass House, USA

The Glass House is a house pared back to its essence. All 'skin and bones', utterly transparent but tiny and unexpectedly cottage-like, it at once highlights and subverts what we consider a house to be. The extreme minimalism of Philip Johnson's 1949 Connecticut home may have come to symbolise American Modernism, but it's the ability to feel part of a landscape that is its defining feature. Johnson was enamoured with the constructed wildness of Paris' Parc des Buttes-Chaumont and neoclassical English gardens, along with the meadowlands of his Midwest childhood; once inside, it quickly becomes obvious that the perfected landscape all around is the real star.

Tours run from May to November each year, beginning in downtown New Canaan; snap up the autumn dates for a particularly evocative fall colours visit.

8 Casa Das Canoas, Brazil

Brazil's greatest architect, Oscar Niemeyer, designed his rainforest home in 1951. It is both profoundly modern and totally of its time and place, Niemeyer here disregarded the architecture of the 'ruler and the square', instead finding inspiration in the plasticity of poured concrete and his immediate environment: 'its white beaches, its huge mountains, its old Baroque churches, and the beautiful suntanned women'. His tropical eroticism is a riot of curves, voids and surprise incursions by the landscape itself: a giant boulder traces a staircase down into bedrock, then rears up to form part of the outside swimming pool.

The house, set deep in the Tijuca Forest on Rio's outskirts, can be visited by appointment: plan your trip at www.niemeyer.org.br.

9 Kunio Maekawa House, Japan

Modernist pioneer Kunio Maekawa's relocated home is a wonderful example of the fertile dialogue of traditional Japanese aesthetics and the philosophies of European Modernism. Built in 1942, its diminutive size, restrained simplicity and clever use of internal pillars owe something to the architect's time in Le Corbusier's studio (he worked on Villa Savoye) along with severe wartime

PHILIP JOHNSON'S
MINIMALIST GLASS HOUSE,
CONNECTICUT

restrictions on materials, but are also typical of Maekawa's innovative spirit and skill at creating bright but intimate living spaces. The original furniture designed by the architect specifically for the house and restored personal objects also remain in situ, these too are an evocative blend of Modernist lines and Japanese craft traditions.

The house is part of the Edo-Tokyo Open Air Architectural Museum, a perfect primer for anyone interested in Japanese architecture from the 17th century to the post-war era.

Top travel lists ● ● ● ● ● ● ● ●   ● ● ●   ● ● ● ● ●

10 Rose Seidler House, Australia

Harry Seidler, an Austrian refugee trained by Breuer and Gropius, designed this home for his parents in the late 1940s. Nestled among bushland in Sydney's affluent northern suburbs, Seidler's 'house of glass and legs' helped shape the future of Australian architecture. It's an homage to his European teachers, yes, but also an Antipodean reinvention of the architect's Bauhaus principles, a clever reworking of the traditional raised houses of coastal Australia. A floating skeletal form is anchored into the landscape by means of a long ramp, sandstone walls and louvred screens, while the light and open interiors remain lovingly furnished with original 1950s furniture and appliances.

Rose Seidler House is open on Sundays and best visited by car. Visit http://sydneylivingmuseums. com.au for location details, as well as details of the annual Fifties Fair. ● *By Donna Wheeler*

Best burger experiences

To celebrate the centenary of the hamburger bun, loosen your seatbelt and come on a tour of the planet's best and most bizarre burger experiences.

1 Slider man – birth of the burger, USA

In 1916, while Europe was in the grip of the Great War, Kansas-based fry-cook-come-inventor Walter Anderson dreamed up something truly great: the hamburger bun. Five years later he opened White Castle, a fast-food joint in Wichita, serving 'sliders'. The USA remains the burger's spiritual home – synonymous with everything that's good, bad and downright ugly about it. Some might say the bad is represented by the gargantuan chains that eventually overran White Castle, but the good is still in evidence in boutique burger bars such as New York's Burger & Barrel, where you can chomp the signature Bash Style Burger, winner of five NY Food & Wine Festival gongs.
Sink your teeth into a slider at Burger & Barrel (25 West Houston St, New York; www.burgerandbarrel. com) or a surviving White Castle Restaurant (www.whitecastle.com).

2 Dromedarian delicacy, Morocco

Camel meat has always featured in Arabic cuisine – camel liver cooked in hump fat is a delicacy in many parts of North Africa and the Middle East – but Morocco's Cafe Clock has become famous on the undulating back of its East-meets-West fusion dish, the camel burger. Founded in Fez, with a sister restaurant now open in the Kasbah of Marrakesh, the venue is a cultural centre where you can listen to local storytellers and music, take cooking classes and do a 'Download' experience – a crash course in all things Moroccan, from mealtime etiquette to basic language skills.
Find the Cafe Clock (cafeclock.com) at 7 Derb El Magana in Fez, and 224 Derb Chtouka in Marrakesh.

3 Arctic explorers, Canada & Iceland

In the challenging climes of the frigid far north, indigenous peoples have survived on a super high-protein high-fat diet for centuries. While few, if any, communities now enjoy a truly traditional diet, many of the meats they've always eaten can still be found on menus, sandwiched betwixt bread buns. In Whitehorse, capital of Canada's Yukon Territories, the Klondike Rib & Salmon's caribou and elk burgers are sensational, while further north, the musk ox burger served at Tonimoes Restaurant in Inuvik is an Inuit treat. In Iceland, Reykjavík restaurants such as Grillmarkadurinn offer burgers from the gourmet – puffin, reindeer – to the highly contentious: minke whale meat.
Tonimoes is in Inuvik's Mackenzie Hotel (www. mackenziehotel.com). See also www.klondikerib. com and www.grillmarkadurinn.is.

SINGAPORE'S HEALTHY
VEGANBURGERS
PROMISE GREAT TASTE
WITHOUT THE GUILT

*At VeganBurg
in Singapore, soya
and mushrooms
are used to create
burgers, livened
up with zesty
pineapple and
satay sauce*

Top travel
lists

IMAGE COURTESY OF VEGANBURG

4 The great British ham'burn'ger, UK

You might expect to find the world's spiciest burgers in Mexico, Sri Lanka or India, but actually, it's the Brits who really relish the red-hot meat experience – taking masochistic masticating to a nuclear level. The Atomic Fallout burger served at the Atomic Burger restaurant in Bristol is so hot that diners must sign a legal disclaimer, wear protective gloves and prove they're over 18 and sober before they begin eating it. Not to be outdone, the XXX Hot Chilli Burger produced by Burger Off in Hove near Brighton, Sussex, registers 6–9 million on the Scoville heat scale (to put that in perspective, Tabasco sauce scores 2500–5000) and has hospitalised several people.

Burger Off is found at 52 Brunswick St West, Hove (follow the screams). See also www.atomicburger.co.uk/ fallout-challenge for more.

5 Kiwi burger, New Zealand

Burgers don't have to be outlandish or enormous to be worth travelling for. Born in the pumping heart of one of the world's true adventure capitals, Queenstown's funky Fergburger serves protein-heavy fodder to fuel you up for any number of bungee jumps, jet-boat rides and zorbing forays. Being New Zealand – where humans are outnumbered 6:1 by sheep – the lamb burger is particularly special, but the Little Bambi Fiordland venison burger is quality too, and the fish (Codfather), beef, and chicken-and-swine combo (Cockadoodle Oink) options don't disappoint either. Wash your choice down with a handle of Kiwi tap beer.

Follow the flock to Fergburger at 42 Shotover St, Queenstown. See www.fergburger.com.

6 Big Bird sandwich, South Africa

Nothing gives you a taste of Africa quite like a mouthful of ostrich, and one of the best places to chase this classic Saffa dish down is at the excellent Neighbourgoods Market that kicks off once a week at Cape Town's Old Biscuit Mill. Housed in a renovated Victorian-era warehouse, this is always a lively spot, but every Saturday it goes into sensory overdrive. Stallholders compete to tempt you towards their steaming pots, bubbling pans and sizzling hotplates, filling the air with foody fragrances from around the world, but we recommend going local and grabbing an ostrich burger from the grill.

The market (www.neighbourgoodsmarket.co.za) runs Saturdays 9am–2pm, at the Old Biscuit Mill (373–5 Albert Rd, Woodstock, Cape Town; www.theoldbiscuitmill.co.za).

7 Bloodless burgers, Singapore

The art of packaging a well-considered patty within a multi-storey bun and splashing it with relishes isn't the exclusive sport of carnivores – there are many great non-murder burgers on menus around the world. Many meathead joints offer veggie options, but the best bloodless burgers are invariably made by dedicated animal-avoiding venues, such as VeganBurg in Singapore. Here soya and mushrooms are used to create burgers, livened up with zesty ingredients like pineapple and satay sauce. Its Paleo Burger goes further, substituting the bread bun with layers of fresh lettuce. The health-kick continues on the side too – with fries sprinkled with seaweed instead of salt, and organic soft drinks.

Find the original VeganBurg at 44 Jalan Eunos, Singapore (www.veganburg.com).

8 Burgers with bounce and bite, Australia

Much of Australia's famously ferocious fauna will take a lump out of you, given half a chance, but it's possible to return the favour at a number of places where crocodile burgers are on the menu. The white meat is an acquired taste (perhaps because humans rarely eat carnivorous animals). Aussies aren't squeamish about serving up some of their cuter creatures between two bits of bread, either, and kangaroo and emu burgers are quite a common sight on specials boards. To try crocodile, emu, kangaroo, barramundi and other meats, Mindil Beach Sunset Market in Darwin is a hard spot to top.

Mindil Beach Sunset Market takes place on Thursday and Sunday evenings (see www.mindil.com.au). Be Game and Aussie Burgers serve various native offerings.

9 Burger noir, Japan

Japanese cuisine is known for precise aesthetics and artistic flair – with a *kaiseki* meal, for example, presentation is as important as taste. Not so, perhaps, with a Burger King meal deal, but the Japanese arm of the fast-food chain caused a sensation when it launched the Kuro Burger range, starting with the Pearl. Kuro means black, and these creations are exactly that – from the bun to the bamboo-charcoal cheese, black-pepper burger and squid-ink ketchup. The Kuro Ninja has a slice of (non-black) bacon added, and the Kuro Diamond is the outrageously flamboyant member of the family, with a lairy lettuce and tomato garnish.

Join the Japanese darkside: www. burgerkingjapan.co.jp.

10 Supersize me, USA & UK

It's an alarming ride, tracing the uglier side of the slider's evolutionary path. Take the horrifically calorific Doh! Nut Burger from PYT in Philadelphia (beef patty, cheese and chocolate-covered bacon served on a glazed donut bun) or the thoroughly bad taste and inadvisable Las Vegas' Heart Attack Grill, where diners don hospital gowns before tucking into behemoth Octuple-Bypass Burgers with lard-fried chips and buttermilk shakes, served by waitstaff dressed as nurses. If you're over 350lbs (159kg), keep eating for free! Perhaps the silliest slider ever, though, was a one-off burger created by London restaurant Honky Tonk. The Glamburger, decorated with gold leaf, lobster and caviar, had a price tag of £1100.

For more (and we mean an awful lot more) visit www. pytburger.com and www.honkytonklondon.com.

● *By Patrick Kinsella*

EPIC BURGERS SERVED KIWI STYLE AT NEW ZEALAND'S FERGBURGER

Top travel ●●●●●●●●●
lists ●●●● ○ ●●●●

Best places to seek silence

When the modern world's constant clamour gets your ears ringing, escape to these quiet spots and silent retreats.

RECHARGE YOUR BATTERIES AT THE ESALEN INSTITUTE IN CALIFORNIA

1 Kartause Ittingen, Switzerland

In a former Carthusian monastery in Switzerland's hilly orchard country, this hotel and farm complex combines monastic peacefulness and modern comforts. While Carthusian monks take strict vows of silence and solitude, visitors to the Kartause enjoy a rather more relaxed and luxurious existence. Spend an afternoon lost in thought in the 'silent room', quietly stroll the garden's thyme maze, wander the ancient cloisters, or join in group meditation. Afterwards, feel free to exercise your vocal chords while enjoying a meal of fresh-baked bread, raw-milk brie, and salads of local herbs and flowers.

Kartause Ittingen is 40km from Zurich in the municipality of Warth. Rooms start at Sfr169 per night.

2 Emoyeni, South Africa

On the slopes of South Africa's Magaliesberg range lies this Buddhist retreat centre ('place of the spirit' in Zulu). Open to Buddhists and non-Buddhists alike, Emoyeni offers a variety of silent and semi-silent retreats. A weekend 'encounter with enlightenment' requires only one day of quiet, while traditional nine-day Vipassana meditation retreats mean no speaking for more than a week. If that's not your bag, just come here on a 'self-retreat' – eat vegetarian meals, hike in the bushveld, explore the library, or walk the garden labyrinth. Talking is permitted except during daily post-dinner 'Noble Silence'.

Emoyeni is about 100km northwest of Johannesburg, accessible by car via a dirt road. Retreats start at about R1200 (US$100).

3 Esalen Institute, USA

Founded in 1962 by a pair of expanded consciousness-seeking Stanford grads, this retreat centre in Big Sur, California, is the mother ship of the New Age movement. Well-heeled bohemians flock here for massages, encounter groups, 'vision quests', and soaks in the world-renowned nude hot tubs. While most of Esalen's workshops are decidedly un-silent – think Gestalt sex therapy, 'shamanic dream healing' and so forth – the institute is famed for its occasional, highly sought-after silent retreats. Spend five days watching the sun rise over the crashing Pacific, eating local, organic meals, meditating and receiving patented 'Esalen massages', all in total silence.

Esalen is a three-hour drive south of San Francisco. Workshops start at about US$405, and go into the multiple thousands.

4 Iona, Scotland

This dot of an island in Scotland's Inner Hebrides has been a spiritual centre for at least a millennium and a half. Colonised by Irish monks in the early Middle Ages, its scriptorium produced some of the most important illuminated manuscripts of the period. Today Iona is dotted with monastic ruins and enormous stone crosses. It attracts thousands of pilgrims each year, many of whom attend retreats in and around ancient Iona Abbey. While most retreats are Christian-affiliated, many welcome anyone wishing to experience quiet contemplation.

The Bishop's House offers week-long contemplative retreats throughout the year.

5 Nyepi Day, Bali

On the Indonesian island of Bali, locals ring in the Balinese New Year by...not ringing anything at all. Nyepi Day, which usually falls in early spring, is honoured by maintaining complete silence from sunup to sundown. Though a Hindu holiday, it's practised out of respect by most non-Hindu locals as well. In addition to no speaking, Nyepi Day means no travelling, watching TV or listening to music, and no working. Do as the locals do, and use the day for contemplation.

Be aware that business and transportation are curtailed on Nyepi Day.

6 Hridaya Yoga, Mexico

Practise your downward-facing dog and tree pose in blessed quiet at Hridaya, a yoga and silent retreat centre on Oaxaca's glorious Mazunte beach. Get your toes wet with a three-day retreat, practise your fortitude with a 10-day session, or go full-on hermit with an invitation-only 49-day solo experience. A full schedule of hatha yoga, group meditation and study of Hindu, Sufi, Buddhist and Taoist texts will banish the boredom that might creep in after a few days of separation from your iPhone. Plus, the landscape – golden-green mountains tumbling down to an agate sea – is so gorgeous, who needs to talk?

Mazunte beach is an 8-hour bus ride from Oaxaca City. Hridaya accommodation ranges from M$60 (US$2.50) for camping to MS300 (US$20) for a private room.

IONA IN THE HEBRIDES HAS WELCOMED PILGRIMS FOR CENTURIES

7 Kielder Forest, UK

An acoustic engineering professor from the University of Salford recently declared a certain boggy hill in this 600 sq km Northumberland forest the quietest place in the UK. But you don't have to wade through the muck to get peace in Kielder Forest. Far from the nearest town, major road or flight path, this is one of the most tranquil corners of England. Hike, mountain bike, watch for osprey, or sail on one of Europe's largest man-made lakes. Or wait till dark and train your telescope towards the spectacular night sky. In addition to being the UK's quietest spot, it's also one of the darkest.

Kielder Forest is 52 miles from Newcastle. There are a number of lodges and campsites.

8 Kyoto International Zendo, Japan

Get Zen – for real – at this traditional Japanese Zen centre. Guests come from all over the world to practice zazen – the art of seated meditation – in the zendo's incense-fragrant wooden buildings, set in the hills outside Kyoto. Silent meditation is only broken by ritual chanting, though chatting is allowed in the evenings in the old-fashioned farmhouse that serves as the sleeping quarters. This is no spa – expect simple meals of rice, pickles and tofu, manual work, and a daily wake-up time of 4.50am. You'll be rewarded with a clear head and new sense of tranquillity.

The zendo is in Kameoka, just west of Kyoto.
A donation of ¥3000 (US$25) per night is requested to cover food and lodging.

9 Franciscan Monastery of the Holy Land in America, USA

Spend a week as an urban hermit at this latter-day hermitage, behind Washington, DC's Franciscan Monastery of the Holy Land in America. The modernist-style cabin is built for one guest, and comes complete with a kitchenette to encourage self-sufficiency. Guests are invited to stroll the grounds in quiet contemplation, though (non-silent) monks are on hand should you have any questions. Apparently Washingtonians are in need of a break from the grind of city living – the hermitage has been almost fully booked since it opened in 2012.

The hermitage is at 1400 Quincy St, NE. Book well in advance by going to www.myfranciscan.org.

10 Vipassana Meditation Retreat, India

The ancient pre-Buddhist meditation technique of vipassana has been gaining popularity among stressed-out 21st-century dwellers. Vipassana, which means 'to see things as they really are', involves silence, stillness, and observing your breath. Practitioners learn the technique at 10-day silent meditation retreats, held at some 160 centres worldwide. Dhamma Giri, in the Indian state of Maharashtra, is one of the biggest. Meditate beneath cyan skies in a golden pagoda with over 400 separate meditation cells, and share vegetarian meals with everyone from cleaners to CEOs. Adherents claim benefits ranging from tranquillity to psychedelic hallucinations to full-body orgasms (!).

Dhamma Giri is a three-hour drive from Mumbai. Courses are held twice monthly.

● *By Emily Matchar*

Top travel lists ● ● ● ● ● ● ● ● ● ● ● ● ● ● ●

Best places to meet mythical beasts

You don't need to brandish a wand to meet creatures of legend. Beyond JK Rowling's fantastic beasts is a menagerie of real-life animals with a mythical pedigree.

1 Basilisk, India

The King of Serpents is more than one of Harry Potter's foes. Storytellers and naturalists told of this baleful man-eating snake, including Pliny the Elder, Chaucer and Leonardo da Vinci. This millennia-old monster may have been originally inspired by the king cobra, an aggressive snake known for its high-arching attack pattern and unsettling, roaring hiss. Steer clear of snake charmers and seek the endangered king cobra in its natural habitat, on a wildlife-watching trip to India's steamy jungles. But keep a safe distance – it's not the time to discover if you, like the bespectacled wizard, can commune with reptiles. *Tour des Sundarbans (www.tourdesundarbans.com) offers eco-village stays deep in the mangroves of the Sundarbans in Bengal.*

2 Dragons, Slovenia

When translucent newt-like creatures were first seen darting through Slovenia's caverns, they were rumoured to be baby dragons. Locals imagined dragons born in the sea could be swept among the rock pools of Slovenia's cave systems. Now we know these blind amphibians as olm, and their remarkable properties are worthy of the legends. They navigate via electrical signals, they can last a decade without feeding, and their surprisingly long lifespan is keenly researched in the hope of shedding light on the ageing process.

Postojna Caves (www.postojnska-jama.eu) has a vivarium swimming with baby dragons. It's an easy day trip from the Slovene capital Ljubljana and is open year-round.

3 Mermaids, the Philippines

When Christopher Columbus first squinted out at a manatee, he sniffed that mermaids were not as attractive as he'd hoped. Columbus may not have been impressed by these cavorting sea creatures but dugongs and manatees take the scientific name 'Sirenia' after the comely Sirens that lured sailors to their doom in ancient Greek myth. Before you chortle that sailors could mistake an ungainly looking dugong – whose closest relative is the elephant – for a mermaid, observe how gracefully they somersault and nose through sea grasses in the Philippines.

Eco-conscious Dugong Dive Center (www.dugongdivecenter.com) offers full-day excursions to their feeding grounds along the Busuanga Coast.

4 Werewolf, Romania

Pointy-toothed counts emblazon souvenirs in Romania's Carpathian Mountains. But it's the *vârcolac*, or werewolf, that truly caused peasants of old to secure their shutters at sundown. The sight of a grey wolf elicits primal fear in many, so it's no wonder that old superstitions surrounded this fearsome predator. And while modern Romanians would sniff at the *vârcolac*, an uneasy relationship with wolves remains. Few wolf attacks on humans have been verified, but nonetheless, media hype puts these mostly elusive canines at risk from hunters eager to cull the threat.

Wolves are shy, so avoid wildlife excursions that 'guarantee' sightings. Maximise your chances by joining a guided nature tour in spring (April to June) and look out for Romania's other fanged beasts, bears and lynx.

5 Kraken, Mexico

Tales of the kraken – a colossal squid with a taste for human flesh – spread from Norway across the seafaring world (getting larger and gorier with each telling). Central and South America have the most vicious real-life kraken. Numerous fishermen have been injured by the saw-sharp beak of the *diablo rojo* (red devil) or Humboldt squid. These carnivorous cephalopods move at 25km/h, form shoals of up to 1000, and flicker red when furious. They can bulge as big as 2m long – not island-sized, as described in the old Norse tales, but certainly large enough to sink your dinghy.

Thrillseeking certified divers can join a guided dive into red devil territory with Big Fish Expeditions (www.bigfishexpeditions.com).

ARMED AND DANGEROUS: GET UP CLOSE TO A REAL-LIFE LEGEND, THE HUMBOLDT SQUID

Top travel lists ● ● ● ● ● ● ● ●
● ● ● ● ● ● ● ●

6 Marine unicorns, Greenland

Compared with their prancing, land-based counterparts, unicorns of the sea have a deliciously dark myth of origin. Inuit lore says that the narwhal came from a woman catapulted into the ocean, attached to a harpoon launched by her son. Brooding on the sea floor, her long hair became twisted into a single horn, and she swam the waves as a narwhal ever after. In the Middle Ages, Greenlanders peddled these tusks – which can grow to 3m long – to Norse settlers as unicorn horn. Whether this was in homage to their mythical origins, or simply to make a tidy profit, we can't be sure.

Northern Greenland's shores in May are your best bet for seeing narwhals; try a wildlife cruise of Melville Bay or excursions from Qaanaaq. Browse a smorgasbord of marine tours on www.greenland.com.

> **Himalayan brown bears could be mistaken for yeti, rumoured to stagger on two legs through the Himalayan mists**

7 Yeti, Nepal

Blame thin air and exhaustion-induced hallucination if you must; but the yeti myth is backed by numerous sightings in Nepal's high passes. Mountaineer Reinhold Messner claims to have had an encounter of his own with the hirsute humanoid. Later – following a 12-year search – he decided it was most likely a type of bear. Himalayan brown bears, which rear up on their hind legs, could certainly be mistaken for yeti, which are rumoured to stagger on two legs through the Himalayan mists. But that hasn't stopped countless yeti hunters from keeping their camera lenses ready, just in case...

Nearly a quarter of Nepal is protected land, so browse welcomenepal.com for your pick of parks and reserves with bears.

8 Kappa, Japan

Don't say a word about those pizza-eating ninjas. The original humanoid turtles are Japanese *kappa*. These folorn turtle-people play childish pranks or (if you're unlucky) wreak misfortune. Fortunately Japanese folklore describes the *kappa* as easily bribed with soba noodles or cucumber. *Kappa* statues grace shrines around Japan, depicting them as gnomes with shells, suggesting these sea spirits are inspired by loggerhead turtles. These real-life *kappa* inhabit the coasts of Japan's subtropical islands, where the sight of them spreads more delight than mischief.

Visit Yakushima Island in May to July to see hundreds of the kappa's cousins clamber ashore to lay their eggs; Inside Japan (www.insidejapantours.com) has dedicated excursions.

9 Thunderbird, USA

Claps of thunder across the Midwest's yawning plains aren't simply an omen of rain. Native American legend tells of the thunderbird, whose beating wings conjure a storm. The bald eagle is the thunderbird's natural relative, and rich with its own meaning. Native American folklore tells that eagles were created from the offspring of a slain monster, transformed into a bird. The soul-stirring sight of a soaring eagle makes it easy to believe the myths. *Check twww.baldeagleinfo.com/eagle/ eagle1.html for nesting spots and viewing points around the Midwest.*

10 *Bunyip, Australia*

Monsters, spirits and mythological creatures are widespread in Aboriginal Australian lore but one that entered the popular imagination Down Under is the bunyip, a terrifying monster with a bellowing cry that was said to inhabit inland swamps and waterholes called billabongs. When the colonisers fanned across the land from the first settlements in Sydney they found regional variations to the bunyip, but they all described a rare bearded, seal-like creature that hid in the water and occasionally lured people to their death.

Bunyips are best spotted when travelling alone, and always in the dark of night, lurking in remote billabongs somewhere on the east coast of Australia.

● *By Anita Isalska*

A BILLABONG IN THE KIMBERLEY, WESTERN AUSTRALIA – TYPICAL BUNYIP HABITAT

DIANA TONNER © GETTY IMAGES

Top travel lists ● ● ● ● ● ● ● ● ● ● ● ● ● ● ●

Best places to elope

Skip big-wedding stress and run away to one of these exotic, quirky or just plain idyllic destinations for a fuss-free private wedding.

A LOVE LESS ORDINARY: A TRADITIONAL PERUVIAN WEDDING AMONG INCA RUINS

1 The Seychelles

There are ultimate castaway islands. And then there are the Seychelles. The talcum powder white beaches and lush, jungled hills of this Indian Ocean paradise drip with romance, and while only residents can get hitched next door in the Maldives, couples need only check into their Seychelles hotel two days prior to tying the knot here (and take their birth certificates). Most hotels offer a variety of wedding packages; some of the most romantic retreats include the Four Seasons Resort Seychelles on the main island of Mahé, Enchanted Island Resort on nearby Round Island, Constance Lémuria Resort on Praslin, and the more far-flung private islands Frégate, North, Denis and Desroches. Just bring your own biodegradable confetti – the Seychelles take sustainability seriously.

The relatively windless months of April and October provide the most idyllic setting in the Seychelles. For a change of scenery for your honeymoon, it's less than three hours to fly to Mauritius.

2 Masai Mara, Kenya

The romanticism of escaping to Africa to get hitched is undeniable, but how on earth would you do it? Trust Richard Branson to come up with an answer. While the mogul's luxury South African safari camp Ulusaba is perfectly set up for larger weddings (such as his son Tom's in 2013), Branson's newest camp in Kenya, Mahali Mzuri,

3 Ærø, Denmark

While the bureaucracy of marrying legally in most European countries renders a quickie wedding next to impossible, you only need proof of identification, proof of entering the country legally (and proof of a previous divorce, if applicable) to wed in Denmark. With its sleepy historical villages, gentle, rolling farmland and beautiful sea views providing the perfect backdrop for weddings, the Danish Baltic Sea isle of Ærø is among the nation's most scenic – and popular – eloping destinations. With a wedding industry worth an estimated Dkr7 million, Æro is part of a region sometimes called 'Europe's Las Vegas' for its quick marriages. *Leave the (minimal) grunt work to Danish Island Weddings (www.getmarriedindenmark.com), which can organise a simple, stylish quickie Ærø wedding from €590.*

4 Andes, Peru

For spiritual seekers looking to make a symbolic commitment to one another rather than a union bound by religion (or law, for that matter), Peru may be just the place. Here, couples can opt for a traditional 'Arac Masin', or Andean wedding, among stunning sacred Inca sites such as the famous ruins of Machu Picchu. Officiated by an Andean priest – who conducts the ceremony in the native Quechua language – the simple but deeply spiritual ritual is designed to invoke the Inca gods to make your love last through eternity. To make it legal, however, you'll have to complete civil marriage proceedings in Peru, or back at home upon your return. *Explore your options with specialists such as Sumaq Machu Picchu Hotel (http://machupicchuhotels-sumaq.com), Eco Adventure International (http://eaiadventure.com) and Sweet Travel Peru (www.sweettravelperu.com).*

The simple but deeply spiritual ritual is designed to invoke the Inca gods to make your love last

specialises in luxe private nuptials. Simply leave it up to the wedding planner to arrange all the legalities of an achingly romantic ceremony for two (and perhaps the odd giraffe) in the northern reaches of Kenya's famous Masai Mara, before enjoying a private dinner under the stars. *Mahali Mzuri is a one-hour flight from Nairobi's domestic airport, followed by a one-hour drive. Three-night intimate wedding packages – including traditional Maasai entertainment – start at US$6705.*

Top travel lists ● ● ● ● ● ● ● ●
● ● ● ● ● ● ● ○

5 Fiji

What you may have to fork out in flights to reach Fiji, you'll recoup in fantastic all-inclusive elopement package deals at resorts across its 300-odd islands. As the wedding capital of the South Pacific, Fiji spoils couples for choice with its abundance of venues, from simple seaside setups and lush junglescapes to exclusive private island hideaways such as Turtle Island, where scenes from *The Blue Lagoon* were filmed, Likuliku Lagoon Resort with its over-water bungalows, and Matangi Private Island Resort, where you can opt for an all-inclusive wedding for less than US$1000 (plus 20% tax) before retiring to your luxury treehouse.
Browse Fiji elopement locations suggested by Tourism Fiji (www.fiji.travel), Fiji Weddings (www.fijiweddings.com) and Bula Bride (www.bulabride.com/fiji-elopement).

6 Gretna Green, UK

When Parliament tightened marriage arrangements in the middle of the 18th century, requiring couples to reach the age of 21 before they could wed without parental consent, the southern Scottish village of Gretna Green became a haven for thousands of English couples running away to marry in secret. With Scotland allowing on-the-spot marriage via a simple 'handfasting' ceremony until 1940, English lovers could duck across the border and literally tie the knot before an irate father of the bride arrived on the scene. Almost 300 years on, the romance of pretty Gretna endures, with a reported 1500 couples married in the town's famous Blacksmith's Shop every year.
Today's Scottish marriage laws, which still vary slightly to English regulations, require a minimum 29-day waiting period for couples to marry.

TRUE ROMANCE: GET SPLICED
AT SOUFRIERE BAY IN ST LUCIA

7 St Lucia

Eloping just about anywhere in the Caribbean is bound to be magical. But when it comes to scenery, it's hard to beat saying 'I do' in the shadow of St Lucia's majestic Pitons. With no residency period, you can simply turn up and do the deed as long as you've applied for a marriage licence at least two days prior. Luxury sister resorts Anse Chastanet and Jade Mountain offer a fantastic list of locations (including underwater!) while the stylish Cap Maison will marry you on a yacht.

Other Caribbean islands that don't require a residency period include Antigua & Barbuda, British Virgin Islands, Bahamas, Cayman, Dominican Republic and Jamaica.

8 Sierra Nevada, USA

Last-minute Las Vegas elopements are legendary for a reason – you don't have to do much more than ask nicely for a marriage licence in Nevada. But if you're not the type to opt for a drive-thru wedding in an Elvis costume at The Little White Wedding Chapel, head upstate. The ski resorts and public parks perched over crystal-clear Lake Tahoe, near Reno, mean scenic views are standard with any marriage ceremony. Emerald Bay, sheltered from the wind by enclosing mountains, is one of the most picturesque locations. Get your license at Washoe Country Bureau, conveniently open until midnight every day.

There's a guide on the city's tourism site: www.visit renotahoe.com/reno-tahoe/what-to-do/weddings.

9 Tulum, Mexico

While it may sound more exotic to elope to Costa Rica or Nicaragua, there is still nowhere easier to have a Latin quickie (wedding, that is) than the equally romantic shores of Mexico. While plenty of resorts are set up for all-inclusive wedding bashes, smaller boutique hotels on the postcard-perfect Riviera Maya, such as Papaya Playa or Be Tulum, (both with wedding planners available to take care of the necessary documentation), lend themselves to a more intimate ceremony. With pristine beaches, the famous Mayan ruins of Tulum, and exquisite turquoise cenotes (sinkholes) all within easy reach, you'll be spoiled for photo opportunities here too.

Mexico only recognises civil marriages, perfect for non-denominational elopers. See http:// papayaplayaproject.com and www.betulum.com.

10 Ubud, Indonesia

Getting hitched legally in most Asian countries can be a headache for foreigners. It's somewhat easier in Bali, but easier still to complete the formalities at home and come here for a romantic traditional blessing ceremony based on Hindu-Balinese customs. The verdant tropical surroundings of Ubud, in central Bali, offer an intimate alternative to the island's crowded beaches, with competitive packages at a handful of luxurious properties. Wed in an orchid garden backed by emerald rice paddies at the Alila Ubud, for example, then pop down to its brand new Seminyak sister resort for your honeymoon.

Plan your nuptials between May and September for the best chances of good weather. See www. alilahotels.com/ubud/weddings. By Sarah Reid

Top travel lists ● ● ● ● ● ● ● ●
● ● ● ● ● ● ● ●

Best moustache destinations

Whether for their menfolk's bold lip plumage or bountiful hairy events, these spots have achieved moustache excellence.

1 Rajasthan, India

A man without a moustache is a rare sight in India's largest state, as having a full-bodied nose neighbour is an age-old symbol of virility here. Which may explain why local gents grow fantastically long 'staches: size matters. It's no surprise the world record holder for lengthiest moustache lives in Rajasthan. If you run into him – and many do in Jaipur – you'll recognise him by his 4m-long mouth brow. Another hot spot for free-flowing facial hair is the annual Pushkar Camel Fair. After some 200,000 Rajasthani farmers finish trading livestock, they vie for follicular superiority in the Moustache Competition.

The 'staches gather for the Pushkar Camel Fair from 8–14 November. See www.rajasthantourism. gov.in for more.

2 Portland, USA

Lip warmers are on display year-round in this burgeoning hipster city, but they ramp up big-time during the week-long Facial Hair Fest in March. The world's only Moustache Film Festival is a star component, screening movies about Salvador Dalí, Jesus, hippies and mountain men, among others. There's a Stash of the Titans contest between moustachioed bands, and a Facial Hair Farmers Market to shop for grooming products. The fest culminates with the Moustache Pageant, where daring noses hit the catwalk and compete in categories such as the Magnum PI (natural 'stache, no wax) for the fuzzy trophy.

For the full schedule of bewhiskered events in late March, see www.facialhairfest.com.

3 Budapest, Hungary

Hungarian crumb catchers are so iconic they get their own category at the World Beard and Moustache Championships. You know the type: big and bushy, starting in the middle of the lip and then sweeping up to the sides. Even the nation's currency celebrates the look, specifically the 20,000-forint note that shows statesman Ferenc Deák in all his hirsute majesty. Budapest remains the centre of the scene and home to the Hungarian Moustache Fellowship. As it notes in its slogan: the Hungarian moustache isn't only hair. Incidentally, paprika – the country's favourite spice – is said to stimulate moustache growth.

Prepare for your visit by watching The Grand Budapest Hotel, *a fun tribute to facial hair.*

4 Trondheim, Norway

This hard-drinking city of seafarers has an epic moustache history. It was Norway's capital in Viking times – home of the very dudes who originated badass whiskers. Viking kings ruled from Trondheim a thousand years ago. Walk around the ancient buildings and walled fortress and you can almost feel facial hair sprout (though it should be pointed out: archaeologists now think the stereotype of wild-bearded Vikings was a myth, as they've found abundant grooming tools in burial sites). Trondheim is also the headquarters of the powerful Norwegian Moustache Club, and it's the only city to host the World Championships twice. *Visit Norway (www.visitnorway.com) has the lowdown on Trondheim's sights; the Norwegian Moustache Club (www.dnm91.no) has the low-down on its lip sweaters.*

5 Istanbul, Turkey

The Turkish moustache is the envy of the world. It's so significant it plays a role in national politics: a large, walrus-style nose accoutrement can indicate left-wing sympathies, while a neat, almond-shape is a sign of a conservative. Around a third of Turkish men have a cookie duster. But what about the guy who can't grow one? There's a moustache implant for that. Istanbul has become the globe's top spot for the procedure. The city also holds the mother lode of tea gardens, where 'staches of all types congregate to sip from tulip-shaped glasses and play backgammon. *Derviş Tea Garden (Mimar Mehmet Ağa Caddesi), opposite the Blue Mosque, offers prime lip viewing.*

A MAN CELEBRATES WINNING 'LONGEST MOUSTACHE' AT PUSHKAR CAMEL FESTIVAL, INDIA

Top travel lists ● ● ● ● ● ● ●
● ● ● ● ● ● ● ●

6 Mexico City, Mexico

We can't overlook the lady 'stache, and no-one represents it better than Frida Kahlo. The renegade artist painted her bold unibrow and moustache in many self-portraits, not giving a fig what anyone thought. The blue house where she lived most of her life sits in the bohemian, cobblestoned neighbourhood of Coyoacán. It's now a museum and pilgrimage site to the heroine of womanly whiskers. Wander through and you'll see Kahlo's outfits, books and paints, as well as the bed where she often was confined due to illness. Under the canopy is a mirror facing down that she used to render her bristled image. *The Museo Frida Kahlo (www. museofridakahlo.org.mx) affords an intimate look at the artist's life and lady 'stache.*

7 London, UK

Do you have a 'hirsute appendage of the upper lip, with graspable extremities'? That's the qualification for membership in London's Handlebar Club. The group formed in 1947 to mark mastery of the wide, thick, ends curved up look (think industrialist JP Morgan or his cartoon alter-ego, Mr Monopoly). The club meets monthly in a Marylebone pub to chew over topics such waxing techniques, moustache cups (specially designed to prevent soup messiness) and snoods (a band to keep the 'stache in place when sleeping). The chaps even publish a sassy calendar showing off their lady ticklers. *The Handlebar Club (www.handlebarclub.co.uk) meets the first Friday of the month; the website has details.*

8 Black Forest, Germany

The region is more than cuckoo clocks, deep dark woods and chocolate-cherry cakes: it's also the cradle of competitive moustache growing. The World Championships were born in the hamlet of Höfen. The nearby town of Pforzheim hosted the second global event, and has long been the home of Germany's national contest. Moustache clubs proliferate and encourage an anything-goes style among members – the Fu Manchu, the pencil-thin villain effect, or mind-blowing free-style arrangements. Perhaps that's why winners of the world contest so often hail from these parts. *The Black Forest Tourism Board (www.black forest-tourism.com) provides information for exploring this moustachioed region.*

9 Liverpool, UK

Liverpool offers a mash-up of moustachery. First, there's the Beatles. The lads famously started out in Liverpool, and the Beatles Story museum tells the tale. View their upper lips through the years and consider whether it's a mere coincidence that their musical peak matches their moustache peak (lookin' at you, *Sgt Pepper*). Nearby the Merseyside Maritime Museum is all about Liverpool's ships and port history, with a bonus of lip toupees. The online 'Moustaches from the Past' exhibit shows company workers who embraced the

'stache, a hardy breed who knew how to 'shave at sea in a gale'. *See the Fab Four's nose ticklers at Beatles Story (www.beatlesstory. com) and Merseyside Maritime Museum's lip warmers at www. liverpoolmuseums.org.uk/maritime (go to 'Archives,' then 'Displays and Online Exhibitions').*

10 Austin, Texas, USA

Austin is home to lots of whiskered dudes who can be seen around town drinking beer and wiping barbecue out of their

Moustache clubs proliferate and encourage an anything-goes style among members

bodacious soup strainers. Most are members of the Austin Facial Hair Club, a ferocious band of competitors that sends more 'staches to world events than any other city. And this year you'll see more of them growing than ever, preparing to twist, curl and wax their hairy regalia into spectacular formations for the 2017 World Beard and Moustache Association's biennial international championships, which will be held here. *The Austin Facial Hair Club (www. austinfacialhairclub.com) has event info. Handlebar (www.handlebaraustin.com) is a moustached-themed tavern downtown.*
● *By Karla Zimmerman*

Top travel lists ●●●●●●●●
●●●●●●●●

Index

BEST IN
TRAVEL
2016

Acknowledgements

Published in October 2015 by Lonely Planet Publications Pty Ltd

ABN 36 005 607 983

www.lonelyplanet.com

ISBN 978 1 74360 745 9

© Lonely Planet 2015

© Photographs as indicated 2015

Printed in China

PUBLISHING DIRECTOR Piers Pickard
COMMISSIONING EDITOR Jessica Cole
COPYEDITOR Bridget Blair
ART DIRECTION Daniel Di Paolo
LAYOUT DESIGNER Austin Taylor
PRE-PRESS PRODUCTION Tag
PRINT PRODUCTION Larissa Frost, Nigel Longuet

WRITTEN BY Brett Atkinson, Alexis Averbuck, Sarah Baxter, Joe Bindloss, Abigail Blasi, Jean-Bernard Carillet, Will Cockrell, Fionn Davenport, Imogen Hall, Tom Hall, Paula Hardy, Martin Heng, Alex Howard, Anita Isalska, Patrick Kinsella, Catherine Le Nevez, Emily Matchar, MaSovaida Morgan, Claire Naylor, Brandon Presser, Charles Rawlings-Way, Sarah Reid, Lorna Parkes, Dan Savery Raz, Andrea Schulte-Peevers, Tasmin Waby, Luke Waterson, Donna Wheeler, Dora Whitaker, Clifton Wilkinson, Chris Zeiher, Karla Zimmerman
THANKS TO Shweta Andrews, Wayne Murphy

Lonely Planet offices

AUSTRALIA 90 Maribyrnong St, Footscray, Victoria, 3011, Australia
Phone 03 8379 8000
Email talk2us@lonelyplanet.com.au
USA 150 Linden St, Oakland, CA 94607
Phone 510 250 6400
Email info@lonelyplanet.com
UNITED KINGDOM 240 Blackfriars Road, London SE1 8NW
Phone 020 3771 5100
Email go@lonelyplanet.co.uk

Front cover image Mount Fuji and Chureito Pagoda, Japan © f11photo/Shutterstock. *Chapter openers:* page 8 Matsuyama, Japan; page 50 Waiheke Island, New Zealand; page 92 Nashville's Riverfront Park; page 134 Grand Prismatic Spring, USA.

MIX
Paper from responsible sources
FSC™ C021741
www.fsc.org

Paper in this book is certified against the Forest Stewardship Council™ standards. FSC™ promotes environmentally responsible, socially beneficial and economically viable management of the world's forests.

BEST IN TRAVEL 2016 starts with hundreds of ideas from everyone at Lonely Planet, including our extended family of travellers, bloggers and tweeters. Once we're confident we have the cream of 2015's travel choices, the final selection is made by a panel of in-house travel experts, based on topicality, excitement, value and that special X-factor. Our focus is on the merits of each destination and the unique experiences they offer travellers.

Although the authors and Lonely Planet have taken all reasonable care in preparing this book, we make no warranty about the accuracy or completeness of its content and, to the maximum extent permitted, disclaim all liability from its use.

GRAZIANO @ GETTY IMAGES

Travel planner

BEST IN TRAVEL 2016

January

Procissao Maritima, Costa Verde, Brazil Ring in 2016 in maritime style in Angra dos Reis, where decorated ships and boats from near and far dock for this carnival-at-sea on 1 January. (Pages 84–7)

Return of the Sun, Greenland After more than a month of continual polar night, Greenlanders celebrate the sun's return in mid-January. Villages throw their own celebrations with cake, coffee and singing as the sun cracks the horizon. (Pages 42–5)

Food & Wine Festival, Punta del Este, Uruguay A festival for gastronomes held in the second half of January in this glam coastal city. It features events, cocktails and dinners hosted by some of South America's top winemakers, chefs and mixologists. (Pages 38–41)

February

Carnaval, Montevideo, Uruguay Carnaval is a big thing in Uruguay's capital, with parades, candombé dance troupes and African-influenced drumming. (Pages 38–41)

Winter Carnival, Kotor, Montenegro Masquerade balls...concerts... generally raucous revelry in February – you could be forgiven for thinking you're in Venice during Kotor's annual Winter Carnival, the biggest date in the calendar this side of Christmas. (Pages 94–7)

Onetangi Beach Races, Waiheke Island, New Zealand A highlight of the Auckland summer social calendar, this 100-plus-year-old event takes places in late February and features races for horses, tractors and amphibious vehicles. (Pages 68–71)